*Encyclopedia of
Fifty Year Old Magic*

Encyclopedia of Fifty Year Old Magic

By

VcToria Gray-Cobb
Geof Gray-Cobb
Maiya Gray-Cobb

The Alternative Universe
Edmonton, Alberta, Canada
www.alternativeuniverse.ca

Encyclopedia of Fifty Year Old Magic
Copyright © 2020

ISBN: 978-1-9991283-5-7

By
VcToria Gray-Cobb
Geof Gray-Cobb
Maiya Gray-Cobb

All rights reserved. No part of this book may be reproduced in any form or by any means, without permission in writing from the publisher.

IT WILL ALL MAKE
PERFECT SENSE
AT THE END.

TILL THEN TRUST AND
ENLIGHTEN YOUR
SOUL ENERGY.

Forward

This book is unlike any other book that you will have read. It will set you up for change. I have taken the best of the best from all five books of my late father, Geof Gray-Cobb and the best of the best from my late Mother, Maiya Gray-Cobb. Plus I have added the much needed astrological signs to be able to proceed under the correct energies.

Read it through to understand what we will be setting out to obtain. As you are reading this book from cover to cover and your intuition nudges you, take a note of the page number. You may be surprised after you have set up the entire working process what may come to fruition from your notations.

Never will we be calling on one being only, UNLESS it is a simple quick desire. No, much like a house is built; contractors are called in to do all the different things needed to make the house whole.

In this book you will have your own personal Seven Angels named for you, coming from your identification. We are using your date, day, zodiac, time and ruler. Your time of birth also includes the Group Leader Angel. This is the ruler of your Angel guides.

Next you will have the option of calling on other Angel helpers with the sign that the Moon will be sitting in. Thus if your requests are not working, you can now try them all over again in each individual Moon sign until you find the correct energy.

All this and more. Allow me to take you through the proper steps to be opening up the gates to the knowledge that so few are able to connect to. We will work with time, energy and YOUR own personal Angels and guides. At times other Angels will be present to enhance the energy when needed.

Other books by Geof Gray-Cobb (AKA Frater Malak)

The Mystic Grimoire of Mighty Spells and Rituals – Here are the most superior Spells and powerful Rituals – the bare bones of magic – set down step-by-step in plain, clear English by Frater Malak. Originally revealed and published by Geof Gray-Cobb in 1976. Re-published in April 2019.
ISBN: 978-0-9812138-5-9

NAP: The Miracle of New Avatar Power – How the secrets of the ancients are able to bring to you the life you are looking for. Follow Geof Gray-Cobb and the knowledge he imparts to you from years of research. Originally revealed and published by Geof Gray-Cobb in 1974. Re-published in May 2019.
ISBN: 978-0-9812138-7-3

Helping Yourself with Acupineology – Through the simple and painless techniques of stimulating the mystic pineal section of the brain, you can direct the energy field that flows around your body to draw to you happiness, health, freedom and money, easily and automatically. Originally revealed and published by Geof Gray-Cobb in 1980. Re-published in July 2019. ISBN: 978-1-9991283-0-2

Secrets From Beyond the Pyramids – Based on his understanding of the awesome power of the Pyramids, Geof Gray-Cobb shows you how New Psychic Energy Power can quickly and easily transform your present existence into a life of deep and lasting satisfaction. Originally revealed and published by Geof Gray-Cobb in 1979. Re-published in October 2019. ISBN: 978-1-9991283-1-9

Amazing Secrets of New Avatar Power – Your mind, body and soul run on New Avatar Power and so does the whole Universe. A follow up to his last New Avatar Power book originally released in 1974, this book was originally revealed and published by Geof Gray-Cobb in 1978. Re-published in January 2020. ISBN: 978-1-9991283-2-6

Other Books

Angels: The Guardians of Your *Destiny* by Maiya and Geof Gray-Cobb. Yes, my father's name was attached to this book as it was my mother's first publication of her works and she chose to add his name. Published in 2008. ISBN: 978-1-9991283-2-6

Seeds Of The Soul by Maiya Gray-Cobb. Published in 2009. ISBN: 978-1-9991283-2-6

Books by VcToria Gray-Cobb

Then Now and Forever – A memoir by Vctoria Gray-Cobb. When you fall in love with a bank robber life is not the same. This intriguing memoir takes you through the life of crime, love, jail, addictions and more. At the age of 21 VcToria met and fell in love with a bank robber. This life not only led to jail, it led to a downward spiral of drugs, depression and the life she had to fight out of to find her true life. Forty years later she decides to look backwards for the true love of her life. What she found even shocked her. Read about all the miracles that happened once she left the old life behind and let the new life begin. First published in 2018 and a newly revised edition published in January 2020.
ISBN: 978-1-9991283-8-8

TABLE OF CONTENTS

1. FIND YOUR PERSONAL ANGELS 1
    Section One.. 2
    Section Two.. 3
    Section Three 3
    Section Four... 4
    Section Five.. 4

2. VISION BOARD JOURNALS AND ALTARS 9

3. BIFURCATED SOUL? DO YOU HAVE ONE? 17

4. REVERSAL SPELL... 22

5. PEACE.. 24
    THE NEW AVATAR POWER IS HERE
    FOR YOU TO USE 27
        What Is This Mysterious Power? 27
    PHYSICAL TENSION MAY IMPEDE
    NEW AVATAR POWER 28
    YOUR CONFIDENTIAL CORPOREAL
    COMMANDS.. 29
    FREEWILL IS OF GREAT IMPORTANCE 31
    HOW TO RELAX PHYSICALLY 31
    HOW TO "COME BACK" FROM THE
    NEW AVATAR POWER RITUAL 35
    HOW TO KNOW WHEN TO COME BACK 35

6. HEALTH 38
    THE WEST FACE OF HEALTH
    AND STRENGTH 40
    THE PEDAL-PATELLA HEALING TRIAD 41

    THE FINGER CONTACT TONUS TECHNIQUE ... 42
        Finger Contact Tonus Technique 43
    THE SUPREME BACK-TO-HEALTH RITUAL 45
    CHANT TO BRING HEALTH 46
7. MOVING 47
    THE IDEAL CHANGE-MY-HOME RITUAL 47
8. MONEY AND MATERIAL 49
    THE VITAL BRING-ME-WEALTH SPELL 49
    INVOCATION FOR MONEY 51
    THE NORTH FACE OF MATERIAL WEALTH 51
9. MONEY MAGIC: AN OCCULT EXPERIMENT .. 53
10. GAMBLING 65
    THE TERRIFIC WIN-IT-ALL SPELL 65
11. BUSINESS 67
    THE INSTANT BUSINESS-SUCCESS SPELL 69
12. LEGAL 71
    THE FANTASTIC WIN-AT-LAW SPELL 71
    INCANTATION TO WIN A LEGAL ACTION 72
13. TRAVEL 73
    THE BRILLIANT TRAVEL-SAFETY SPELL 73
14. ASTRAL TRAVEL 74
    ASTRAL TRAVEL 74
15. ASTRAL TRAVEL BOOK 76
    BIOGRAPHICAL SKETCH 76
    INTRODUCTION 76
    WHAT IS ASTRAL PROJECTION 78
    HOW IS ASTRAL TRAVEL PERFORMED 78
    IS IT DIFFICULT TO ASTRAL TRAVEL? 79

OUTLINE OF THE METHOD 80
PREPARATIONS FOR ASTRAL TRAVEL............. 83
SURROUNDINGS 83
YOUR PHYSICAL BODY 84
BEST TIMES TO TRAVEL 85
SUMMARY OF PREPARATIONS 86
RELAXATION 87
SEEING YOUR ASTRAL BODY 89
HAND SEEING 89
SEEING THE COMPLETE ETHERIC BODY 91
SEEING YOUR OWN ETHERIC 92
SEEING A PARTNER'S ETHERIC 93
PHYSICAL CUE TRAVEL..................................... 95
MENTAL CUE TRAVEL 98
FUTURE PROGRESS 100
VARIATIONS ON CUE TRAVEL 101
RETURNING TO YOUR PHYSICAL BODY 101
EXTENDING YOUR JOURNEYS 102
WHAT NEXT? 103
ASTRAL TRAVEL IS SAFE AND ENJOYABLE ... 104
SUMMARY 106
CUE 1 108
CUE 2 110
CUE 3 112

16. LOVE, LOVE, LOVE...................................... 115
THE EAST FACE OF LOVE AND
PEACE OF MIND 115
DISPEL LONELINESS WITH THE MAGNETIC

PICTORIAL TECHNIQUE 116
17. ENERGY ENHANCING.. 119
   Your Psinic Field... 120
   Your Pectoral Field.. 120
   Your Umbilical Field 120
  GESTURES BRING YOUR ENERGY FIELDS
  UP TO MAXIMUM STRENGTH......................... 120
   Your Umbilical Gesture..................................... 121
   Your Pectoral Gesture 122
   Your Psinic Gesture 122
   Performing More Than One Gesture 123
18. CHANNELING... 124
19. ANIMALS 127
  LOST PET 127
   Instructions 128
   More Instructions 128
  SICKNESS IN YOUR PET.................................... 130
20. DREAMS 132
  DREAMS AND WHAT THEY CAN TELL YOU..... 132
   Astral Traveling In Dreams 133
  PAST LIFE DREAMS 136
21. ALIENS AND SPACE SHIPS 140
22. PENDULUMS, TIPS AND ADVICE 144
  GENERAL PURPOSE INVOCATION 144
  THE DIFFERENCE BETWEEN RITUALS
  AND SPELLS... 145
   Rituals... 145
   Spells 145

 Pendulum Work 145
WRAP UP 146
PHASES OF THE MOON 149
 New Moon 149
 Waxing Crescent Moon 149
 First Quarter Moon 149
 Waxing Gibbous Moon. 149
 Full Moon 150
 Waning Gibbous 150
 Third Quarter 150
 Waning Crescent 150
TESTIMONIALS 150

CHAPTER 1

FIND YOUR PERSONAL ANGELS

Taken from *Angels: The Guardians of Destiny* by Maiya and Geof Gray-Cobb published in 2008. All rights to this book are owned by VcToria Gray-Cobb

You have seven Angels that will personally work with you. Let's get to figuring out who they are.

I chose to design a deck of 86 Angel cards that are specifically created for this book. They have all the information that you need to work with on all of the days, months and not only that, the exact time of the workings. These cards are available for sale on my web store on: www.alternativeuniverse.ca

If you choose not to purchase the cards you must create either 122 names on 86 separate papers or 122 separate pieces of paper. You may separate these or copy the theme.

The date of your birth is section one.

The month of your birth March 21st to April 20th and all other months are in section two.

Aries and Mars are together, as are all the zodiac signs and their rulers in section three. We have two Angels on this card.

The actual day of your arrival is in section four.

The time of your birth and Group Leader are on one card. Again you may separate these, or follow the theme. Section five.

If you follow the theme you have 86 cards and if you choose to have paper for each individual Angel then you will have 122. Use the boxes and section numbers to create the cards/paper for yourself if you are not buying the designed cards.

- ❖ For the date of your birth refer to Section One

- ❖ For the month of your birth refer to Section Two

- ❖ For the sign of your zodiac and ruler refer to Section Three

- ❖ For the day of your birth refer to Section Four

- ❖ For the hour of your birth [if your hour is unknown you will use Noon] and Group Leader refer to Section Five

Section One

Date of Your Birth:

1st	Lahabiel	16th	Madin
2nd	Ahariel	17th	Diniel
3rd	Samael	18th	Ygail
4th	Shahriva	19th	Adroni
5th	Valnum	20th	Miton
6th	Anael	21st	Veruah
7th	Ahiel	22nd	Jesod
8th	Sadquiel	23rd	Neciel
9th	Azar	24th	Sadayal
10th	Aban	25th	Todros
11th	Johiel	26th	Astrad
12th	Seth	27th	Tufiel
13th	Tir	28th	Sebastien
14th	Katspiel	29th	Alesimus
15th	Tatriel	30th	Miniel
		31st	Astel

Write down the Angel's name or find the card bought in the 'Angel' deck.

Section Two

Month of Birth:

March 21st	– April 20th:	Favardin
April 21st	– May 20th:	Asmodel
May 21st	– June 20th:	Leybel
June 21st	– July 20th:	Imrief
July 21st	– August 20th:	Afsi-Khof
August 21st	– September 20th:	Morael
September 21st	– October 20th:	Elogium
October 21st	– November 20th:	Ahadiss
November 21st	– December 20th:	Ophiel
December 21st	– January 20th:	Nadiel
January 21st	– February 20th:	Ausiel
February 21st	– March 20th:	Isfandarmend

Write down the Angel's name or find the card bought in the 'Angel' deck.

Section Three

Ruling Sign	Angel	Ruling Planet	Ruling Angel
Aries	Malahidael	Mars	Ertosi
Taurus	Bagdal	Venus	Eurabatrus
Gemini	Sariel	Mercury	Pi-Hermes
Cancer	Cael	Moon	Pi-Joh
Leo	Verchiel	Sun	Pi-Re
Virgo	Iadara	Mercury	Arista
Libra	Zaniel	Venus	Hagith
Scorpio	Riehol	Pluto	Ambriel

Sagittarius	Sarataiel	Jupiter	Zachariel
Capricorn	Haniel	Saturn	Kafziel
Aquarius	Archer	Uranus	Azel
Pisces	Rasamasa	Neptune	Joel

Write down the Angel's name or find the card bought in the 'Angel' deck.

Section Four

What day of the week were you born? If you do not know, just Google your birthdate for the day.

Sunday:	Hurtapal
Monday:	Curaneil
Tuesday:	Hyneil
Wednesday:	Miel
Thursday:	Sachiel
Friday:	Sarabotes
Saturday:	Machatan

Write that Angel's name down in your list or find the card bought in the 'Angel' deck.

Section Five

Now for your time of birth. As stated above if you do not know it, use Noon. Later you can choose different cards to work with different times and see if you get a better success rate. That way you more than likely will have figured out your true time of birth.

If you were born at:	Your Hour Angel:	Your Group Leader:
1:00 am to 1:59 am	Arathiel	Gamiel
2:00 am to 2:59 am	Praxil	Farris

FIND YOUR PERSONAL ANGELS

Time	Angel	Group Leader
3:00 am to 3:59 am	Crucial	Sarquamich
4:00 am to 4:59 am	Phorsiel	Jefischa
5:00 am to 5:59 am	Patrozin	Abasdarhon
6:00 am to 6:59 am	Prenostix	Zaazonash
7:00 am to 7:59 am	Anapion	Mendrion
8:00 am to 8:59 am	Hanoziz	Gastrion
9:00 am to 9:59 am	Adrapen	Nacoriel
10:00 am to 10:59 am	Mameroijud	Jusquarin
11:00 am to 11:59 am	Adjuchas	Dardariel
Noon to 12:59 pm	Darmosiel	Sarandiel
1:00 pm to 1:59 pm	Charmeas	Soluzen
2:00 pm to 2:59 pm	Labezerin	Anael
3:00 pm to 3:59 pm	Parmiel	Vequaniel
4:00 pm to 4:59 pm	Aclahaye	Vachmiel
5:00 pm to 5:59 pm	Camasayer	Sazqhiel
6:00 pm to 6:59 pm	Medussusiel	Samil
7:00 pm to 7:59 pm	Librabis	Barquiniel
8:00 pm to 8:59 pm	Iphun	Oscaebiel
9:00 pm to 9:59 pm	Kirtabus	Vadriel
10:00 pm to 10:59 pm	Chorob	Oriel
11:00 pm to 11:59 pm	Rosabis	Bariel
Midnight to 12:59 am	Voizia	Beratiel

Write down the Angel's name or find the card bought in the 'Angel' deck.

Add the hour Angel to your list and as you will note the cards have the Group Leader Angel named. If you are designing the names with paper add the Group Leader to this paper.

You will now have five Angel cards with seven Angel names. These are your personal Angels. They will always be the group that you use in all of your magic workings.

An example is: I am born on a Sunday so one of my Angels is Hurtapal. I am born on the 12th so that Angel is Seth. I am an Aries ruled by Mars. That card has two Angels, Malahidael and Ertosi. I am now looking at the month of when I was born and Angel Favardin is another. My time of birth is 4:26 am and Angel Phorsiel represents that. Also on this card you find the Group Leader who takes care of these six Angels, mine is Jefischa.

These five cards should remain separated from the other 81. Keep them next to the deck or on top of the deck. As you take your place at your altar to work these five cards must be placed around your work first. Use four to place South, North, East and West with the Group Leader card always sitting above. You will note that this is the only card that you have to pay attention to so that it sits upright. All the others are created with a double energy and can never be in a reverse position. This was done on purpose so that nothing can go wrong.

Before we start I wish to add a few comments. Back in the late 1970s moving into the 1980s the world was very prejudice. Being anything but your own sex was frowned upon, abortions were illegal in many places, the church still took a strong position for many and so much more was frowned upon. Thus in the days that the books I refer to were written, the choice of using Magic, pendulums, tarot cards, angel cards and more was advised to be kept silent. Particularly Magic.

Today the world has moved passed a lot of silly nonsense. Therefore if you wish to keep your altars, visions boards and journals lying around your home please do so. If you wish to discuss the outcomes of your magic workings feel free to do so. Create your own groups to enhance the energy if you are all working towards the same goal. All magic and intentions that you put out into the Universe is your own energy. It no longer needs to be silenced.

However, if you feel like keeping your work private and to yourself, feel free to make that choice. Either way, whatever works for you keep that as your tradition.

I wish you well with all of your future shifts, magic and change. As long as I walk this physical plane I will send out the energy to all the magic workers under the Pisces Moon as I have done for all who still connect to my late Fathers work. I have also blessed the Angel cards, plus all items that now sell on my web store that enhance the work of the books.

If I have left the physical plane then know that if possible I will always look down upon you as you travel the journey and help if I can.

You do not need to own these books, but it will help, as I do refer to them at places in this book. The value of owning books when the original author has passed from the physical is sometimes astronomical. As you can see when you Google these books.

Recommended to own:

- ➢ *The Mystic Grimoire of Mighty Spells and Rituals* by Frater Malak AKA Geof Gray-Cobb. Originally revealed and published by Geof Gray-Cobb in 1976. Re-published and slightly re-edited in 2019.

- ➢ *The Miracle of New Avatar Power* by Geof Gray-Cobb. Originally revealed and published by Geof Gray-Cobb in 1974. Re-published and slightly re-edited in 2019.

  ➢ *Secrets From Beyond The Pyramids* by Geof Gray-Cobb. Originally revealed and published by Geof Gray-Cobb in 1979. Re-published and slightly re-edited in 2019.

  ➢ *Helping Yourself with Acupineology* by Geof Gray-Cobb. Originally revealed and published by Geof Gray-Cobb in 1980. Re-published and slightly re-edited in 2019.

  ➢ *Amazing Secrets of New Avatar Power* by Geof Gray-Cobb. Originally revealed and published by Geof Gray-Cobb in 1978. Re-published and slightly re-edited in January 2020

I have not re-published these last two books by my late mother, but you can if you wish Google them and find them under second hand books. I will not be re-publishing them.

  ➢ *Angels: The Guardians of Your Destiny* by Maiya and Geof Gray-Cobb. Yes, my father's name was attached to this book as it was my mother's first publication of her works and she chose to add his name. Published in 2008.

  ➢ *Seeds Of The Soul* by Maiya Gray-Cobb. Published in 2009.

CHAPTER 2

VISION BOARD JOURNALS AND ALTARS

Once we have our group of Angels we will set them aside for now as we build our own personal vision board. You have several choices here.

If you dedicate a small room to your magic work then building an altar to do the work is preferable. Having a vision board is the next best thing to an altar. You will work with that. You will need two journals.

If your space is small then you can just use two journals. One titled 'Now' and the other titled 'Destination'. You will need these in the beginning so purchase them or put together paper so that it is stapled and creates a book.

Why two journals? One is your life now and one is the life you are about to create with the magic, energy shifts and all that is suggested to you as we travel this wonderful soul journey.

Words for you to choose from: Read these words and see if you tend to allow yourself to feel or use any in the negative sense. You then write out the negative and place them in the area you have named 'Now'. Then, taking the positive write them out and place them in the 'Destination' area.

Positive	**Negative**
Idealistic	Egocentric
Belief	Paranoid

Positive	**Negative**
Sensitivity	Narrow vision
Sense of security	Suspicious
Harmony	Overbearing
Dependable	Egocentric
Compassion	Lack of understanding

Positive	**Negative**
Physical energy	Overbearing
Spiritual knowledge	Impatient
Self reliant	Intolerant

Positive	**Negative**
Self-possessed	Over analysis of self
Spiritual aspiration	Stubborn independence
Resolves relationships	Competitive

Positive	**Negative**
Harmony	False judgment
Respect	Over emotional

Positive	**Negative**
Intuitive	Vain
Self-awareness	Unrealistic
Humanitarian	Resentful

Positive	**Negative**
Gentility	Morose
Acceptance	Cold

Positive	**Negative**
Love	Clinging
Understanding	Depressive
Practical	Controlling
Sensuous	Insecure

Positive	**Negative**
Self-responsibility	Over analysis
Sharing wisdom	Too logical
Intuitive	Secretive and closed

Positive	**Negative**
Calm	Need for joy and hope
Aspirational	Aloof
Regeneration	Unfriendly

Positive	**Negative**
Vitality	Uncertainty
Euphoria	Confusion
Romantic	Moodiness

Positive	**Negative**
Determination	Temperamental
Endurance	Spiteful
Humane	Glum

Positive	**Negative**
Imagination	Arrogance
Charismatic	Exhibitionist

Positive	**Negative**
Wisdom	Egotistical
Self-expression	Opinionated
Satisfaction	Feeling inferior

Positive	**Negative**
Perfection	Discouraged
Happiness	Frustrated
Cosmic love and truth	Self-indulgent

Positive	**Negative**
Mental activity	Mental tension
Ability to rationalize	Anxiety/depression
Concentration	Superficial
Confident	Opinionated
Optimistic	Deceitful

Positive	**Negative**
Passion	Suppression
Power	Anger
Personal Will	Vindictive

Positive	**Negative**
Caution	Uncommitted
Compromise	Closed off

Positive	**Negative**
Knowledge	Martyr
Contemplative	Unrealistic

Positive	**Negative**
Peaceful	Lack of harmony
Generous	Envious/jealous
Feels free	Stubborn
Contented	Cluttered mind
Persevering	Resist change
Confidence	Self-doubt

Positive	**Negative**
Dependable	Judges self
Organized	Stubborn/rigid
Conscientious	Irresponsible
Responsible	Feels unwanted

Positive	**Negative**
Independent	Inhibited
Creative	Lacks self-worth
Sociable	Self-pity

Taking your first journal aptly named 'Now' you will write. Write honestly about how you see your life in the emotional, spiritual, material and physical way.

What types of emotions are holding you back? Do you 'need' approval all the time to be motivated? Are you jealous of other people's lives? Have you been ridiculed in the past and carry it now? Are you in a demeaning relationship and feel helpless? Emotions are felt from within and create the outer sense of the journey. Be honest as you bring them to the surface.

Spiritual feelings? Do you meditate daily? If not we can guarantee you do not have the maximum progress that is available to you. What percentage do you feel is your intuition right now? Do you want to let go of beliefs that do not suit you now? How enlightened are you? Add any other notes that you feel are related to your spiritual life.

Material. How much do you have? Write down every material thing you own. Vehicle, furniture, job, money, home and all that you have bought, inherited or just have kept over the years in a material sense.

Physical: How is the health? Write down your maladies that are holding you back from creating the perfect life. Admit it if you are a hypochondriac or others tell you this. Admit it if you hold onto these illnesses only because you get attention and otherwise would not. Add the emotions to the emotional area if this is how you feel. Is it weight you wish to lose? Write down how much.

If there is any other area that you wish to shift, grow into, change, then add it to your first journal. From this point on the word 'Now' will refer to this journal.

Move to the second journal that will be referred to as 'Destination'. Open page one of 'Now' and create page one in 'Destination' as you would like to see it. We are working on a 365 day schedule to envision where you would like to see yourself in one year, but better still what memories do you wish to have? From the 365th day we will have a destination course that will swing you into a life that has purpose, growth, meaning, happiness and best of all 'that which is yours to live'.

From here I will be placing suggestions from the best of the best from all of Geof Gray-Cobb's books under each title chapter.

I prefer if you start this journey on your birthday. Why? This is the most powerful time of the year. Your Sun sits back in the position that it was in when you first entered into the earthly plane. The

Sun of course is the power behind your destiny. If you use the power of your Sun position to its maximum potential you will be miles ahead of those around you.

However, if you are saying "damn, my birthday was last week, do I have to wait a year?" No, you can start at any time but I feel that the effort put in as a birthday gift to yourself is wonderful. But start at any time. Just date it in 'Now'. In 'Destination' put the date but mark it for exactly one year later to the day you begin.

While you are setting up all of this, look around for pictures of places you want to have as memories as a travel destination. Now recall we are only working in a year time frame so do not place 100 pictures in your pile. Take anything that you feel would be something that you would like to have whether it be a new home, new car, new body, new enlightenment, new relationship, just about anything that you come across in photos, pictures or online visuals.

We tend to see better when creating visuals with our eyes closed. However, if you feel that you can visualize a lot more by viewing a picture then use that method. However, with our vision boards or altars we will be looking at them daily. If you are using the altar make sure you go and look at it daily or meditate in front of it. Connecting with the eyes of the soul awakens growth. Growth creates destiny and destiny is the journey. As we reach our final days on the earth plane we do not want regrets, but further more we do not want to get to the other side and say "damn, I have to repeat all that"?

I would prefer to work with an altar. This way you have the place of peace. Everything is in one area and you enhance the energy each time you sit before the altar and meditate. If you can, place a chair there so that it is easy to walk in and start the magical energy shift. Also you will leave the 'Destination' journal on top of it once you are done the daily enhancing of energy.

We begin with finding your complete soul.

CHAPTER 3

BIFURCATED SOUL? DO YOU HAVE ONE?

Time: If you are able to start on your birthday then activate this then.

Next Best Time: Sun Sign: As long as you use one of the Moon times any Sun sign is fine.

Pisces Moon at either 7 am, 11 am, 7 pm or 11 pm in your own time. No other Moon placement holds the correct energy.

Bifurcation means the splitting of a main body into two parts. Everyone must take responsibility for the quality of their thoughts, behaviors, and actions. With today's energy and the creation of man's thoughts towards the changes that reside in each, we tend to lose ourselves. Our true selves. We feel we must believe what the majority wants. We must follow the crowd so to speak, and yet we know it is not what we truly want. Our energy leaves us. We exist, but are not happy. We have lost some of who we are.

Energy can never be destroyed it can only be reshaped and reprogrammed. So, before we launch into the spells, chants, magic, shifts and all that is of tremendous power, we must bring our full selves to the light of where we must work from.

Begin by sitting in front of your altar or the place you have chosen to work your magic shifts. Have your 'Destination' journal beside you. Place your 5 'Personal Angel' cards or paper if that is what you have written their names on, in a circle. If you have chosen to create all your 'Personal Angel' cards on separate paper then you will have 7 pieces of paper to set forth.

Place them on the altar, or in your working space. Now bring in all of the other cards or paper with the names that I trust you have neatly printed out and place them intuitively around your seven personal Angels.

This is a vital step and not to be taken lightly. If you have little time, then come back later. You are only setting this up once and it needs to be done properly. You are calling in all of the light of your soul that is either hidden in darkness, despair or simply never been put to use due to fear or conditioning from the outer world of energies that others send your way.

Light a candle, pink if possible but white, cream, indigo or purple will also do well. Not black or any other dark colors. Incense is nice, but not necessary if you do not like sweet smells or smoke. If you are using incense, use sandalwood or myrrh.

Now, as the candle burns and the smell of incense moves through the energy, call each of your seven personal Angels' names out loud. Call on the Leader first.

If by chance any of your Angel cards move slightly please rearrange them. This is the Universal energy not liking the placements on the altar or your magic working place of choice.

Now looking at the rest of the cards/paper bring the names to your mind one at a time and say each out loud. You have a choice here. You can name all of the 115 Angels [you are not calling on your Personal 7 here] and announce the following paragraph to all of them OR take the time to address each individual Angel.

Naturally if you take the time to address each individual Angel not only will they hear you they will feel a delight in being addressed singularly. Yes, this will take about an hour or so but the power to work with this full energy will be explosive as you move forward. You decide how much you want to create with your life.

If you choose to do the 'group' calling do not miss any of the 115 names. Taking each card or paper and announcing the Angels name and putting it aside will ensure this.

At this point either call all 115 names and then use the following paragraph OR call upon one name and use the following paragraph and repeat with each name 115 times [Note that 115 adds to 7 the spiritual number]. Putting aside each card/paper as you complete the words.

> I, [state your full given name] born [state your full date of birth] in [state your location of birth] under the astrological sign of [state your sign] at the known time of [state time of birth] ask that you evoke me with all of the Universal plan, energy and journey that has been set forth for me to obtain with all of the information I have supplied.

Now you address your Seven Personal Angels.

> I now call upon, [say each of your personal Angels names] to bring in the seven energies that have been created for me. I ask that each Angel that has been assigned to me, now reach out into the Universe and bring back all that has been lost from my program of life. I

ask that all energies be absorbed back into my material body and that this journey set forth now not be disturbed in any way other than the light bringing forth the experience that I gratefully acknowledge and accept. I take this pact with the Universe and I trust that my life now will be the one of which my initial map of DNA was created for.

Next and this is very important. Leave all of that which you have set up and lie back. Whether you are sitting or laying it matters not. Close your eyes and give permission for the energy shifts to take place. Quieten your mind, do not think any thoughts. If you do, disregard them as you feel them surface and only focus upon your breathe. I will not give any time frame here for this final action. When you feel full of life, or a shift of intenseness, or perhaps a voice, a whisper or any shift that now tells you to open the eyes then do so.

Say 'thank you' with immense gratitude as you put your cards/paper together. Blow out the candle and allow the incense to burn away.

Lastly we will now send our Angels home till we call upon them again. These words are to be used at the end of any sessions. Do not forget. They will not leave until you are ready to have them go. If you forget to allow them to go back, other work that they have to do will suffer. The words you will speak out loud after you have expressed your gratitude will be 'ETA MESA EST'. These are magical words and once you have recognized the shift of energy that arrives as you call your Angels, you will learn to feel them leave.

This next action will really enhance the journey. Take a pot and a small plant, just a seedling that clearly has germinated. A nice plant, one that you feel would look great in your décor. Put soil into the pot, plant the roots into your pot with determination that this plant, as it grows, will show you when the journey shifts. Every time you look at it and see new growth you will know that your energy is shifting. This is also your 'gratitude gift' to the Angels who have just set your true life in motion.

Now, any energy that has been lost has come back to you and we will move onwards towards fulfillment.

One last enhancement is to take all of the 86 cards/paper with all of the 122 Angels and sleep the night with them. This is a way of getting to know the energies that will be yours to work with. A strong bond is formed as you work each day with the individual energies that are formed in the cosmos. My advice is to sleep for seven nights with all of the cards. Separate the seven Personal Angels and sleep with them on the left and the other 115 on the right. Yes, you may leave them in their golden sacks.

Note: The golden sacks refer to the cards if you bought them. If you are using homemade cards you may wrap them in anything gold.

CHAPTER 4

REVERSAL SPELL

Sun Sign: Obviously you will have chosen the sign that sits with the spell you wish to reverse so again any Sun sign.

Moon: should be sitting in Scorpio for this reversal. You may also use Aquarius.

I have put this near the beginning of the book so that you will not have to worry. In my e-mails and readings of people who activate the desire to make shifts, sometimes they cannot handle the miracles that now start to happen. Some see it as bad luck, some see it as unwanted. Some cannot handle the shifts. Some are just not ready, even though they thought they were. Some will absolutely refuse to budge and will go into depression. We do not want you to take any journey that you had perceived yourself as ready for, but when the train left the station you were not happy with the journey.

Here is the reversal spell. This will take you right back to where you were when you activated what you thought you wanted/needed/desired etc.

Using your Seven Angels, take the four cards that do not have the Group Leader and lay them sideways. By this I mean you can still see the picture but the name is laying left to right. If you are using paper then the same action applies. Now take the Group Leader card and keep it upright and place it above all four.

REVERSAL SPELL

Simply say with any color candle lit "I apologise for wasting your time, I was not ready to create change" Say the name of the Leader Angel and then say "please instruct all of the helpers of the Angel group to remove all the energy shifts that were done for me. I invoke my request and ask for immediate assistance".

Lie back, breathe in and hold for 30 seconds thinking of one name of one of the six Angels. Do this another five times with each of the names. Sit up, thank the Leader Angel by name and DO NOT FORGET to say ETA MESA EST.

Now go about your life. Whatever you felt was not for you has been reversed.

Warning: Once you have reversed whatever you felt you couldn't handle as it came to you, do NOT activate this again for at least one year. If you do call upon the Angels for whatever you choose to reverse make sure you are ready. This spell only reverses ONCE. It will reverse any actions, but only each one ONCE.

If you create the same spell/magic/chant/again the Universe will not reverse it as your personal Angels will acknowledge that subconsciously you do want what you fear and will make the changes no matter what.

CHAPTER 5

PEACE

Sun Sign that is best: Any sign. Meditation should be done daily.

Moon signs: As this will be done daily you will feel certain days that are more in tune with your own energy than others. I do a 'group' meditation under a Pisces Moon once a month. I post the time on Face Book under my thread The Alternative Universe plus Geof Gray-Cobb.

For myself I connect strongly under the Pisces Moon but you will be meditating under all Moon signs.

In this chapter I will be using the meditation from *The Miracle of New Avatar Power* by Geof Gray-Cobb. I will be using the creation of peace with a bit of modification from *Secrets From Beyond The Pyramids* by Geof Gray-Cobb. All five Angel cards will be used so that the seven Personal Angels assist.

I feel in infinite wisdom that once you attract 'peace' all else follows. I wrote my own memoir in regards to this, realizing that once you let go of what you know is not making sense, then the map of life is created for you. Therefore I truly ask that you do the journey with my suggestions in the order of which I created just for you, the reader.

From the book *Secrets From Beyond The Pyramids* by Geof Gray-Cobb

In this book it gives you instructions on how to build the pyramid plus the offer of purchasing one, already colored with all of the symbols for South, East, North and West. After constructing the pyramid or buying one already made, set it up with East facing you. The Blue Circle of Vayu is attached to the East side on the ready-made pyramids and this too faces you.

At all other times the pyramid will face east but if you have more than one I ask that you put one on your altar or vision board. This will enhance all of the actions to arrive peacefully.

In your magic working space or altar, place a picture that is cut out of a magazine, downloaded from the internet or any photo of a person in meditation. To me this is the best visualization of 'peace' in the moment.

Arrange your seven personal Angels around the area that you have chosen to place the pyramid. Since we are working with five cards I suggest that you place them facing the four directions of North, South, East and West with the Group Leader leaning upon the east side of the pyramid. Yes, it would be standing upright.

If you do not have the pyramid then simply place them in the four corners of North, South, East and West. Then place the Group Leader above, leaning on a crystal.

Now what is the zodiac sign today? If your date of working is the 2nd of June then you would be taking the zodiac card of Gemini. If you are a Gemini, then you already have this card as one of your Personal Seven Angels. You do not need any other card. But if

PEACE

you are an Aries or any other astrological sign then you would be adding Gemini.

Announce their names in a greeting of 'choice'. One of my Angels is Seth. I will use him as a reference throughout the book when I need to show examples. "Good Day Seth" or "Good Morning Seth" are two ways of greeting each Angel. Make sure you are using the names of your own personal Angels.

Because this is such a powerful shift I am going to call in helpers for you. Why? Think of a house being built. Once the foundation is laid, the contractor in charge will then start to call in different journey men or woman to start the piping, dry wall, electrics, painting etc. etc. Each of these makes the house stronger and more complete. We do not use them all the time, but they are on the list for hiring when work of their caliber is needed.

Now, what day is it today? Look for the Angel that relates to this. However, if it is Sunday and you were born on a Sunday, you would already have the Angel card ready. But if it is Monday then you will be adding Monday's card.

Now what date is it today? If it is the 2nd of the month and you were born on the 2nd of any month then you already have the strength of that Angel. However, if the date is the 25th then look for that card and add it to the work area.

Now move to the month. Take that Angel card and place it in your work area. Again, if you are born in June and it is June then have the Angel helper. If it is any other month you are working in then find that card.

Lastly look at the time zone area and note what time you have chosen to work. You should now have an extra five cards. Four, perhaps three if any have already been taken as your own personal Angels.

As you place them use your intuition as to where they may like to lay. Greet them as well by name. Always keeping your Leader Angel above the laying of all cards. If you feel so inclined you may introduce the cards of the day to the Leader first, and then if you still feel inclined, to the other six Angels. Ask that they work together for the laying of the ground work. Remember all you are asking for is INNER peace. Not anything else.

VIP: When you pick the time card there will be another Group Leader added. Do not stand this Group Leader up.

Your Group Leader Angel should always be the one to sit prominently beside the East facing pyramid. However, make sure you introduce both Leaders and use the word Leader when addressing either.

Sit back and pick up *The Miracle of New Avatar Power* by Geof Gray-Cobb [the revised edition published May 2019] and turn to page 8. There you have the New Avatar Power ritual. You may either use this as it is spoken, or used my updated version that sits with your personal Angels.

THE NEW AVATAR POWER IS HERE
FOR YOU TO USE

You should understand that everyone has Avatar Power. The only difference between an unsuccessful frustrated person and a happy successful person is that the successful one has tuned in to his Avatar Power – either by accident or design.

What Is This Mysterious Power?

Quite simply, it is what the Ancient Egyptians, the Essenes, and many other ancient races of men used to call "The Power of the Mysteries." It is the same Power that was sought in the Middle Ages by witches, warlocks, sorcerers, theurgists, and alchemists.

Yet those magical researchers of the Middle Ages were only partly on the right track. Many of their accessories, some of their chants and incantations, tools, spells, alleged Words of Power, and other ingredients were totally unnecessary. In fact, most of the old magical books contain a great deal of useless material that was put there *merely to confuse the layman.*

Now, after years of occult research, I have found out which are the useful pieces of the old spells and rituals, and which parts can be safely discarded without affecting the desired end results. From that research I have put together the necessary parts of the Avatar Power working in a form that anyone can use.

The result is that, with the help of this book, you can now work any miracle you wish.

PHYSICAL TENSION MAY IMPEDE NEW AVATAR POWER

Taken from *Amazing Secrets Of New Avatar Power* by Geof Gray-Cobb (page 48)

The foaming, exhilarating tide of Cosmic Energy operates like any other flow of natural energy or fluid. It seeks the line of least resistance: it would rather flow "downhill" than "uphill," and if it meets an obstruction it will divide and flow past, rather than wasting vitality trying to go through.

You're tuning yourself to be a channel for Cosmic Energy, and if you represent an obstruction to the easy flow of the energy, it will tend to bypass you, and you'll have less than you should to work your life-changing miracles.

Several ways exist for you to impede this tide, but the primary cause can be physical. In order for your mind to shape and control Cosmic Energy, your physical body needs to be relaxed.

The reason, briefly stated, is that every muscle in your body gives off electric currents when that muscle is tense, and when many muscles are tightly tied in knots, the resulting surge of random electricity somehow interferes with the free flow of Cosmic Energy.

So whenever you start out to work with *New Avatar Power*, your first action is to relax physically. That's the main theme of this chapter, and mastering the simple technique which uses what I've called your *Confidential Corporeal Commands* will automatically and easily open you up as a Cosmic Energy channel.

YOUR CONFIDENTIAL CORPOREAL COMMANDS

Taken from *Amazing Secrets of New Avatar Power* by Geof Gray-Cobb

No need to be scared of that 29-letter title. You're going to *use* it, not have to say it. What does it mean? *Confidential*: secret, personal, for your eyes and ears only. *Corporeal*: material, physical, bodily. *Commands*: authorize, control, rule.

You're about to discover, then, a personal bodily control which is applied by saying or thinking a few simple words.

I have added this action to simply enhance the relaxation that is needed to command the inner planes to work with you. I have shortened this up considerable from the book as I found it long and tedious in explanation.

What's your first name? Not necessarily the one on your birth certificate. You may have been named Stanley or Elizabeth by your parents. Chances are most people know you as Stan or Betty.

You've selected your name. Now what's the first letter, the initial, of your *family* name? Single or married name: your *present* name – the one you sign on a cheque or banker's draft. The name you filled in when you ordered this book. The name you write when someone says, "Please sign here."

The third part of your *Confidential Corporeal Commands* is one word. That word is **Relax**. And the fourth and last part consists of the numbers from 1 to 10.

Putting together the whole of your *Confidential Corporeal Commands goes:* "Ten – Relax (Name, Initial) – Nine – Relax – (Name, Initial) – Eight – Relax (Name, Initial). . . " and so on down to ". . . One – Relax (Name, Initial)."

In place of "(Name, Initial)" you will, of course, use your own name and initial letter we've just arrived at. Algernon Witherspoon, from the example above, would begin: "Ten – Relax, Rick W. – Nine. . ." and so on.

That's your complete and individual *Confidential Corporeal Commands.* Say yours over a couple of times to get the hang of it. Realize that no one in this wide world says those words *exactly* as you do. A product of your own mind, those *Commands* are personally custom-built to have maximum effect.

VcToria Comments: My name is VcToria Gray-Cobb and I use "Ten – Relax, VcToria G.," "Nine – Relax VcToria G.," and so on till I hit number one.

This is a personal way to relax as stated by Geof. I have added several ways, and you may choose to use them all at once, use a different one each day, or pick and choose as you desire. The most important thing is to remember that relaxation connects to the inner subconscious that then guides us to the correct usage of energy and life then rearranges itself.

FREEWILL IS OF GREAT IMPORTANCE

Whoever created this Universe we exist within gave us all a priceless gift, to use or misuse as we wish.

That gift is *free will*: the ability to decide to do something, or not to do it. Free will is part of your life-changing New Avatar Power methods.

So what's the solution? Act or don't act on information received through New Avatar Power? My advice is to follow up on anything which New Avatar Power hands you: if it comes from a New Avatar technique then, by definition, it's designed to lead you towards happiness.

HOW TO RELAX PHYSICALLY

A few short, simple steps separate you from entering a limp, relaxed state. You are about to learn to relax every muscle in your body, and it will take up just 15 minutes of your time each day.

Try to find 15 minutes *every* day for your New Avatar Power Ritual. Ideally, it should be at the same time and in the same place, seated on the same piece of furniture.

Yes, you are going to relax sitting down. Later you will be lying flat on your bed, performing true miracles with your New Avatar Power, but for the moment you should use it while you're sitting in a chair. This powerful Ritual will send you straight to sleep if you practice it lying down at this stage of your development.

Find a place where you can be undisturbed for about a quarter of an hour. Switch off the TV and radio. Turn off the cell phones and any other things that make noise. Decide which chair you will sit in: if it is too soft, you'll fall asleep. On the other hand, if it is too hard you will be uncomfortable. An ordinary padded kitchen or dining chair is excellent.

Place your chair in the room where it feels right for you. Against a wall, in the corner of the room, in the center of the room, by the door, by the window – anywhere: but when you sit down you should feel at ease. Most people choose to place their chair against a wall, facing the door.

Once your chair is positioned, use that spot each day during your New Avatar Power Ritual.

Darken the room by drawing the drapes or hanging a blanket at the window. Ideally, the room should be dim enough so that you cannot read the fine print of a newspaper – but it should never be pitch black during these sessions.

Some people find that a single candle burning, or a dim, colored lamp helps them.

Now arrange a single light to shine gently over your shoulder on to your lap so that you are able to read the New Avatar Power Ritual.

Sit back in your chair. Make yourself comfortable with your back straight, but not stiff. Tuck your buttocks into the back of the chair so that your spine is upright, with your chin held level without any straining to hold the position. Your head should balance easily on your shoulders without any tendency to drop either forward or backward.

Place your feet flat on the floor, almost touching. Loosen any tight clothing you may be wearing. What you wear is unimportant, as long as you are comfortable. You can be barefooted, or even totally nude if you wish.

Lay your hands in one of two ways, whichever feels easier. Either palms upward on your thighs or palms downward on your knees. This is the position you should adopt at all times during the Ritual, except when you are holding this book to read the necessary words.

You are now ready to start.

⦿ "I am beginning the New Avatar Power Ritual. I call upon my Angels to witness. Now you will name all of your seven personal Angels. Name the leader first. Then the next six, and then the daily helper Angels you have brought in. I now state my purpose thus: ANKAR YOD HAY VAW HAY.

"I begin to wind down, to let go and be rid of all the tensions of my body. To let my muscles relax, unwind and let go.

"The tensions are beginning to drain from my body. Soon, a gradual heaviness will start to weigh down my thighs, my arms, my hands, my feet, my legs, my body.

My muscles unwind and let go. All my muscles are relaxing, unwinding, and relaxing.

"Very soon I shall feel the unwinding, the letting go. Unwinding and letting go. Unwinding, letting go. Unwinding. Letting go.

"Deeper and deeper . . . letting go . . . unwinding and letting go.

"The tensions drain from my muscles and they will soon become loose, letting go, relaxing and unwinding.

"Breathing easily and deeply. Easily and deeply.

"Unwinding and letting go . . . drifting into the peace and serenity of complete relaxation. And as my body unwinds and relaxes, so I enter the peace and quiet, where only these words have meaning, and nothing else disturbs me.

"Letting go . . . unwinding . . . letting go . . . unwinding . . . relax . . . relax . . . relax . . . let go . . . let go . . . let go . . . relax . . . relax . . . relax . . . let go . . . let go . . . let go.

"I call on Thee, Mighty Arzel, who stands in the East, to assist me in this and all my ventures. I know now that my New Avatar Power is flooding to the surface. ◉

I now close my eyes gently."

Now sit quietly letting your mind wander as it will, until you feel a deep feeling of white light peace. You will not forget this feeling. Then you may open your eyes.

You may use the CD *Journey of the Mind* by Geof Gray-Cobb in place of reading this above meditation. Listen to both sides. The CD is for sale on my web store or on an MP3 file also on my web store.

If you do not feel the deep penetration of white light peace that you will instinctively know it is that, then try again the next day. Do it daily until you have achieved this 'feeling'

Once completed the pyramid will always sit facing East until you use it again. I also prefer one beside your bed.

The above mentioned FULL session will take place once a week for the next 52 weeks. Recall that we have set a yearly growth opportunity.

HOW TO "COME BACK" FROM THE NEW AVATAR POWER RITUAL

As you practice the Ritual and its spells, you will slip deeper and deeper into a peaceful, relaxed state. Each session will take you further along the path – yet, in an emergency, you will always be able to come back instantly, fully alert, to the real world.

However, provided no one calls you or nothing urgent requires your attention, you should return from the Ritual slowly and peacefully. No harm will come to you if you snap out of it for any reason, but the effects of the Ritual and spells will be more permanent and more immediate if you use the following method of ending your Ritual.

When you have finished working your spell, or carrying out whatever magical business you decided to perform, tell yourself that you are ending the Ritual.

In your mind, say: "Coming back . . . I am coming back, slowly and peacefully. As I count slowly from one to five, I shall return to the real world, feeling well, happy and alert, fully awake, and recalling everything that has gone on."

Then count slowly from 1 to 5, feeling yourself drifting back to the reality of your room. At the count of 5, open your eyes, enjoying the feeling of power and relaxation that will be still with you.

Think for a few moments of what you heard, saw and felt during the Ritual, and then record it in your journal.

HOW TO KNOW WHEN TO COME BACK

As you begin to drift into the peace and serenity of the Ritual, say to yourself: "I shall return in 15 minutes time. My Inner Mind will keep track of the passing minutes and I shall return when the time is up."

After a few sessions reminding yourself of that, you will find that you automatically return to reality on the 15th minute of the Ritual.

You then repeat your "Coming Back" words, become fully alert, write up your results in your journal, and that's it until the next time.

If you wish to add more minutes to your return time do so, or you can simply request 'when you feel the best time for me to return make it aware to my subconscious and let the words "Coming Back" start to flow automatically'.

VcToria comments: It is not my intention to copy any of the books that I have re-published. I am only taking the best of the best. I wish to add though, that in the newly re-published book *NAP: The Miracle of New Avatar Power* by Geof Gray-Cobb on pages 63 to 74 you have another ritual of opening other gates of energy. If you have the book and prefer to use this method please go ahead.

Do not forget to say ETA MESA EST as you complete this energy shift. If you care to make notes of what you have experienced, please be my guest. There is nothing nicer than once your 365 day journey is completed, than reading back to the changes that you felt as you released the negative, and created the positive.

If you prefer to do any other type of meditation at your altar just follow the instructions for setting up the Angels. This is a vital part of the year program. Any time you work anything in this book you must have your five cards that represent the seven Personal Angels. Four is the grounding energy of the four corners of the Universe as you place them. The Group Leader, who is always placed seated upwards, oversees the six Angels, creating a power energy of seven that is the spiritual energy/work number.

In 2011 I attended a six day event at Whistler in British Columbia, Canada with Deepak Chopra. The event was aptly named Seduction of Spirit. Here is where I was first introduced to Primordial meditation. Suffice to say I knew this was the meditation that vibrated to my soul at this point in my life. To this day I still use the activation daily.

Prior to finding the meditation that spoke to my soul I moved through many activations. I started out with cassettes on guided meditations. One of my favorites back then was *The Healing Waterfall* part one and two. I then studied under Buddhist Monks, who offered a nine month, 5 day a week, free study of meditation. Part way in I discovered that not only did these monks smoke cigarettes but the head monk, an 81 year old, also ate meat. I dropped the course like a hot potato. Once you are vegan you will understand that energy shifts tremendously. My belief and it is my belief, is that you cannot teach me anything, nor heal me in any sense if you eat meat. Our energies are not to be meshed. Please do not judge that until you become a vegan and then you decide.

CHAPTER 6

HEALTH

Best Sun signs to work under: Virgo, Taurus and Libra.

Moon signs to work under these Sun Signs: Virgo, Taurus and Libra.

I am covering this now as you cannot have good health if you are not peaceful. Being peaceful means you feel no stress and allow the Universe to bring to you the life you have designed prior to arriving in physical form and proceed with faith from there.

All will agree with me that of course food is the first and foremost necessary daily activity. I would however like you all to give a thirty day try to vegan. Why?

I was born in England and the Brits sure love their fried food. At least when I was growing up they did. I had bacon fat sandwiches to take to school, fried eggs and bacon PLUS fried bread fed to me each morning before I left. On Sundays it was the roast beef, Yorkshire pudding, gravy and then for dessert there was the mandatory treacle pudding or trifles. Can you say UNhealthy?

As an adult I continued with the way we ate and slowly came to realize that food was my medicine. Having said this, it is only to show you that I was not born into a vegan or vegetarian way. I evolved into it, and with this shift came an extraordinary energy around me.

I cannot explain this energy any other way than you feel lighter, more evolved and although life may have shifted it has shifted in a solid way. You connect more to the Universal energy where all the knowledge lies. You do not become so obsessed with the material. You understand that life is taking you on an inner journey, not an outer journey that so many people think is the only way to happiness.

I can only ask, as I have done above, for you to google online vegan recipes. Join a vegan group on Face Book or, if this is a book that is now very old, and you are reading it somehow in whatever fashion tech has chosen to go, there will be much out there for you to invest your time into learning to feel this joy of vegan eating. Unless, if you are reading this in, perhaps 2040, and vegan is now normal.

Who knows? The future may be such that, just like fur coats, eating meat is seen as revolting. I do see it that way now. I feel that the Universe thanks you for understanding that animals are here to show you pure love, not murder.

Now for those who wish to add to the Universal journey of health lets set up an energy course so that it will blend with the 'peace' as all energies are different. Energy can never be destroyed; it can only be reshaped and reprogrammed.

For this shift I ask that you fast as long as you feel comfortable. Also this is best done in the morning or after you awaken. Therefore you have many hours of fasting already done. Now if you can add to this instead of eating then great. If not let's start the sequence of change. Please feel free to drink water at any time prior or during this magical shift of health.

Before you start you need to ask if you truly want good health. Many do not. It is a time when they get attention. It stems from childhood where they were only given attention when they were sick. This could be for many reasons. Too many children in the household, a single parent home that seems to be so fashionable now, or the 'I am too busy' that I hear constantly like it is a medal being pinned on one's lapel. Either way the person who has only received attention when they feign illness or were actually sick gets love. This is inbred into the subconsciousness and now the adult keeps this as doctors and people pay attention to those who complain about feeling ill. If you sit in that category you need to own it and 'want' to shift it or nothing will change.

If you are unclear about where you sit use a pendulum to ask. Ask if you are really sick? Ask if it can be cured? Ask if you can help this along?

How to use the pendulum? I will add these notes at the end of the book.

Let's assume you are ready to be healed.

As above, get your journal and sit at your altar or place of magic working. Get the five personal Angel cards ready. Place them as you have done before and either use the pendulum to ask if you need helpers or not. If the pendulum indicates yes then follow the above instructions. Use the day, date, month, zodiac sign and actual time of working. Again keep your own Personal Group Leader card standing and lay the helper down. Introduce the two. With these extra cards you have up to six more Angels stepping in to help.

THE WEST FACE OF HEALTH AND STRENGTH

From *Secrets From Beyond The Pyramids* by Geof Gray-Cobb

Take the pyramid and use the west side daily. At night pour a glass of water and let it rest against the west side of the pyramid. If you are doing any type of juicing in the mornings you can add the glass of water to the juice or simply drink it as is. This will set a healthy energy day with the energy strictly focusing on your health. If you wish to refill the glass and drink the water hourly this too will be extremely effective. If you can do this practice and follow it with the following action there will be more power going towards your health.

We move back to *Secrets From Beyond the Pyramids* by Geof Gray-Cobb. On the west side of the complete pyramid that is sold on my website store, the Silver Crescent has been added to the beauty of the energy. Once you have completed your meditation open your eyes and focus upon the West Side. Place your cards around the pyramid. Focus once more with the intention of creating perfect health. Your Group Leader card can stand up on the west side.

Make yourself comfortable and close your eyes. By now I hope that you have memorized the New Avatar Power Ritual or decided what meditation is best for your daily routine of the thirty days that brought you the white light peace. The subconscious is being programmed to accept all positive energy that will allow change to manifest under these actions so being repetitious is a huge bonus.

There are two things we will choose from here once your meditation has been completed. If you are mobile we will be doing *The Pedal-Patella Healing Triad* from page 105 of *Secrets From Beyond The Pyramids*. If you are not overly mobile we will activate The Finger Contact Tonus Technique.

THE PEDAL-PATELLA HEALING TRIAD

The *Pedal-Patella Healing Triad* arranges your body to create a solid and powerful pyramid with the lower trunk and limbs.

HEALTH

Lie flat on your back with your legs together. If you're lying on the floor, put a pillow or other pad under you buttocks and another cushion under your head. If you can arrange yourself north and south, with your head pointing to the north, so much the better – but this is neither essential nor critical to this routine.

Keeping your legs together, raise your knees and put your feet flat on the floor. Move your feet toward your buttocks as far as you can *without straining any muscles*. Take it slow and easy and stop the movement the moment any tendon complains!

Now edge your feet apart about 12 inches or so, until, by raising your head you can see your heels as you look past the curve of your hip. Keep your knees touching each other, fold your hands comfortably across your chest and you're in the *Pedal-Patella Healing Triad* posture.

THE FINGER CONTACT TONUS TECHNIQUE

Sitting, standing, kneeling, lying – you can adopt this *Finger Contact Tonus Technique* in any bodily position as long as your hands are free to touch each other.

In a manner akin to the way an acupuncturist alters the energy flows of the body with his needles, this hand posture balances metaphysical energies to help your West Face techniques reach quicker attunement with natural healing powers.

I'm about to describe how to place your fingers, but this is a clear case where one picture is worth a thousand words.

HEALTH

Finger Contact Tonus Technique

Look at Figure 1 and you'll see how to place your hands to achieve the *Finger Contact Tonus Technique.*

Hold your hands a few inches apart, palms facing. Hold your fingers straight, and keep them all as straight as feasible throughout.

Figure: 1

Move your hands together until you can touch the tips of your thumbs together and the tips of your little (fourth) fingers likewise.

Place the tip of your left forefinger against the tip of your right *second* finger.

Then place the tip of your left second finger to the tip of your right *third* finger.

You now have two fingers left over which are not touching their tips to other fingers. They are the third finger of your left hand, and the forefinger of your right hand.

HEALTH

Swing these two fingers down to touch the *base* of their opposite number on the other hand – your right forefinger touches the base of your left forefinger, and your left third finger touches the base of your right third finger.

Straighten out any fingers which you may have bent while putting this together. Check against Figure 1 to see that you've got it right. This is your *Finger Contact Tonus Technique.*

Again this will be done once a week until you feel that your health is increasing or depressions lifting. I will keep reminding you that this is a 52 week journey.

VcToria Comments: I am not a doctor of any kind. I do not claim to be and will never advise you not to follow your own doctor's advice.

I have however cured myself of many aches and pains, unsettled energy and other annoying factors of my own making that created a somewhat unpeaceful way of life. This book is to lead you into a path of total harmony with the one almighty Universe. You can do it, just allow the lessons to be incorporated.

Tips:

Try the vegan for 30 days. If you find a liking to it then stay on that course. For me this was the most powerful shift of energy in my health and mind.

Do the meditations daily along with the belief that all energy will shift for you. Keep focused upon your journey. Do not let others invoke what they feel you should do upon you.

You will need the Amulet Kit to perform any Rituals. They are available for purchase on my web store in color or black and white.

With a bit more effort, as Rituals tend to be that way, here is a very powerful health Ritual.

Taken from the *The Mystic Grimoire of Mighty Spells and Rituals* by Geof Gray-Cobb

Note: These Rituals must not be used in the place of recognized and regular medical treatment. They should be used only in conjunction with your doctor's diagnoses, recommendations and prescripttions. Do not reveal to any medical person that you are performing the Rituals in this part, nor must you make any claims that Magic cured you when you return to health.

THE SUPREME BACK-TO-HEALTH RITUAL

The Ritual banishes general indispositions and brings glowing health and strength. If you have a specific disease, use the Secret Disease-Banishing Ritual which follows this one.

1. Arcane Admitting Password: IAOTH [pronounced "Ee-Ah-Oat," emphasis on the final syllable].

2. The Purpose of Your Call: "My purpose is to regain a healthy state."

3. Planets Represented: Saturn and Mercury.

4. Name of Cosmic Being: MUMIAH [pronounced "Moo-Me-Ah," emphasis on the first syllable].

5. What You Wish to Achieve: "I wish to regain my health and be free of .... [Name the indispositions you wish to banish].

HEALTH

6. Avatar Mantrum: ISH-LEE-AH

7. Best Time of Working: Friday, during daylight hours *or* at 10 p.m., Moon waning from Full to New.

8. Mystic Talisman: No. 6.

CHANT TO BRING HEALTH

Taken from *NAP: The Miracle of New Avatar Power* by Geof Gray-Cobb

1. I call thee Zoroel and Sabriel* who hath dominion over physical and mental health. At my command, banish from me** all diseases, discomfort, sickness, and malfunction of body and mind.

2. Send down Thy beneficial healing rays, for Thou art able to bring this to pass. During each passing hour Your powers will bring youthfulness and freedom from pain.

3. I seal this command with the healing words EEM-AHN-YOU-ELL which Shadrach, Meshach, and Abed-nego sang in the fiery furnace and were delivered. Thus shall Your powers dispel this sickness and disease. So mote it be.

* Pronounced ZO-ROE-ELL and SAH-BREE-ELL.

** If you wish someone other than yourself to be healed, say his or her name instead of saying "me."

CHAPTER 7

MOVING

Sun Sign that is best: Taurus, Leo or Cancer

Moon signs: Done under the above Sun signs. Taurus, Pisces, Cancer or Sagittarius.

> Taken from *The Mystic Grimoire of Mighty Spells and Rituals* by Geof Gray-Cobb

Bring out your five Personal Angel cards and set them up in the four corners, with the Group Leader either up against the North side of the completed pyramid, or any crystal. Now add three zodiac cards to your circle. They must be Aries, Virgo and Gemini. Here you will see you have added Mars and Mercury. Corresponding with the Ritual energies. Now as you call in Purah introduce the Group Leader to him. Then simply say the names of the other Angels noted on the cards and introduce Purah.

Note: You are introducing Purah to the Group Leader. "Purah meet Jefischa" would be my introduction. Then say all the other Angels' names one after each other and say "meet Purah". Now start the ritual.

THE IDEAL CHANGE-MY-HOME RITUAL

Best results are achieved when you know where you wish to go. However, if you have no new home in mind, Purah will locate one for you. Naturally, you will deal with the physical arrangements for moving your belongings. Also remember you are seeking happiness in your new abode: its physical dimensions may not measure up to what you were expecting; Purah, however, is aware of the future and may decide that you will find happiness in a small apartment and only misery in a mansion.

1. Arcane Admitting Password: PHATIAL [pronounced "Far-Tea-Ale," emphasis on first syllable].

2. The Purpose of Your Call: "My purpose is to move to a different home."

3. Planets Represented: Mercury and Mars.

4. Name of Cosmic Being: PURAH [Pronounced "Poor-Ah," emphasis on second syllable].

5. What You Wish to Achieve: "I wish to leave my present abode and find happiness in another one" [If you have a new home already in mind, say so, giving the address].

6. Avatar Mantrum: POO-ROO-SHAH.

7. Best Time of Working: Sunday, 9 p.m. to 11 p.m. or during daylight, close to New Moon.

8. Mystic Talisman: No. 8.

CHAPTER 8

MONEY AND MATERIAL

Sun Signs: Best worked under Aries, Taurus, Capricorn and Cancer.

Moon Signs: Best to work under the above sun signs – Aries, Taurus, Capricorn, Cancer and Sagittarius.

I tend to keep in mind the saying 'you cannot take it with you'. I have never had the desire to do something over and over again just to 'perhaps' one day reach a time in your life when 'maybe' the house will be paid for, 'maybe' you will get a pension, 'maybe' your health will be still be great, and so many 'maybe's'. I believe that you will always get what you need, and sometimes what you want, if you do not worry. Inner peace is so much richer and that is why I focused upon that first.

However, this is a book with a lot of magic inside. Coming from myself, my late father and my late mother. I have also promised you works that I have not re-published at all.

THE VITAL BRING-ME-WEALTH SPELL

Taken From *The Mystic Grimoire of Mighty Spells and Rituals* by Frater Malak AKA Geof Gray-Cobb

This simple Spell has proven extremely successful for hundreds of users. It is concerned with bringing moderate amounts of money to settle existing debts.

MONEY AND MATERIAL

As soon as possible after waking in the morning, write down on a piece of paper what bills need paying or what you want the money for. Keep it simple – write something like: "I need $1125 to pay the rent next month" or "I need $184.50 to bring my charge card payments up to date."

When you have written down your need, draw a line right around the statement. Keep that paper in your purse or pocket for at least 10 hours. Read it as often as you can during the day, *when you are alone and not observed.*

After darkness has fallen sit alone in a room and light a single candle. If you wish you can burn a stick of incense and have music playing. Put out all lights except the candle and read your piece of paper once more.

Then say:

> "Beyond this light the Powers come
> "To bring me this needed sum,
> "Aided by a Cosmic Name
> "Because I burn this Magic flame"

(If there is any likelihood that anyone would overhear you, just say the rhyme in your mind).

Repeat the rhyme until you have said it three times in all, then extinguish the candle. Tear your paper into tiny pieces and throw them away.

Repeat this Spell each evening for seven days or until the money comes, whichever is sooner.

INVOCATION FOR MONEY

Taken From *NAP: The Miracle of New Avatar Power* by Geof Gray-Cobb

1. In the Power of the Names EH-HEH-YEH, YEH-HO-VO-EL-OH-HEEM and YEH-HO-VO-AH-VAY-DAH-ASS I place this Invocation with Thee, Nitika,* Genius of Wealth.

2. Know that I require and command Thee to bring me gold. Thou hast dominion over wealth and Thou shalt begin this very instant to shape the future such that money shall come to me, enough and to spare, by the powers of these Words and Invocation.

3. Be Thou ruled by me in the Names SHAH-DYE-ELL-KIGH and AH-DOH-NIGH-HA-AH-RETZ. So mote it be.

* Pronounced KNEE-TEA-KAH

THE NORTH FACE OF MATERIAL WEALTH

Taken From *Secrets From Beyond The Pyramids* by Geof Gray-Cobb

Our material world is built on the power and stability of the number four. The ancients saw everything composed of the four "elements" – Earth, Air, Fire and Water, and the four 'qualities' – hot, cold, wet and dry.

We fix our positions in the world with four directions – north, south, east and west. Our measurements of material things depend on the four attributes of length, width, thickness and duration.

MONEY AND MATERIAL

We spend much of our life between four walls. The sacred cross, with all its spiritual and mystic powers, has four arms.

A pyramid stands firmly on its base of four sides, usually arranged to face precisely north, south, east and west. Both occult and scientific researchers have shown us that the act of creating a pyramid does something wonderful to the local space-time continuum. For natural reasons which we have yet to fully unravel, building a pyramid focuses unseen energies.

To enhance any of the money spells, rituals or actions concerning the material we will use the North side of the pyramid.

The Completed Pyramid is available for sale on my web store: www.alternativeuniverse.ca. It has been created with all four sides corresponding to the North, East, West and South with additions of the diagrams matching the directions.

As you call upon your Angels and helpers, place the cards around the pyramid so that the Leader Angel card rests upright beside the North side. If you can sit with yourself facing South so that the energy of the pyramid faces North all the better. As before, look at the day, month, date, zodiac and time you are working and pull in the extra help. Keep the Group Leaders apart. One lies down and your Personal Group Leader is standing. Introduce everybody but do the Leader's introduction first.

CHAPTER 9

MONEY MAGIC: AN OCCULT EXPERIMENT

From *Money Magic: An Occult Experiment*
by Geof Gray-Cobb

I have added this here because it sits under the material. I use the number four in many of my business areas. Four is stability. Four is grounding. Four is a number that I always say, funnily enough; to my clients when they are in a Personal Year Four [related to Pythagorean Numerology] "what you foundate in a four year is like the pyramids, virtually indestructible". I have said this for the past 25 years as I read my clients. This book bodes well with this saying.

While Geof Gray-Cobb lived in Montreal, Quebec, Canada in the early 1970s he wrote for Globe Communications as an Occult Research Editor. One of his weekly columns invited his readers to partake in 'Exploring the Occult' a paranormal experiment.
After researching old and new occult texts, he wrote a simplified magical ritual designed to bring the performer of it a $10 bill, and he invites his readers to try it and inform him of the results.

The ritual was published in three weekly instalments. Shortly afterwards, Geof Gray-Cobb received letters from all parts of the U.S alleging that after performing the ritual, money came to the ritualists in unexpected ways.

"Gray-Cobb makes no claims for any occult powers contained within in it, but presents it as a curiosity of the paranormal which seems to have convinced many people that ritual magic can be performed with success by almost anyone."

Ever since I read a magic spell in an old book when I was a youngster, I've been fascinated by Witchcraft and Magic. My question has always been: "Is it for real or not?"

I'd like you to join me in an experiment, if you will. This is going to take up a few minutes of your day, but if we can get results, then one of my pet projects will have been proven beyond a doubt – and you'll have done yourself a bit of good, cash wise.

What I propose is that we carry out one of the old spells, and see it in action. It's quite simple. We're going to start off from square one, and follow the practice of the old sorcerers to produce a $10 bill – by magical means.

VcToria Comments: This was written before 1971. Today I suggest you choose a bill with whatever denomination you wish to attract and follow the magic of this energy.

I hasten to add there that we're not going to ask His Satanic Majesty to exchange our souls for money, and neither are we going to do anything to offend the currency regulations. No one is going to ask you to set up a printing press in your basement either.

We're going to do our best to focus the Cosmic Powers, each one of us, so that a $10 bill arrives in our wallet or purse – by some totally unexpected means.

We'll start small the first time. After it's worked for you, and you believe it, you can carry on to greater heights. But please note one thing: there will be no flashes of lightening, no clouds of purple smoke, no rustle of angels' wings – just natural laws, which you could call coincidence, working to produce what you have magically requested.

Call it coincidence if you like, but when it works for you three, four or more times, you have to start believing that something more than chance is working with you.

I've tried to sweep away much of the confused mishmash which shrouds many of the old magical texts. I've sorted out what seem to be the significant bits, and strung them together into a 28-day magical exercise which anyone can handle. And the end result will be a crinkly $10 bill – or any other sum of money which you feel you can handle.

Lastly, let me add that I've invented nothing new here: I've drawn on old and new manuscripts to put this together.

So you can see that this $10-bill spell is a refinement of the way the old sorcerers used to work. My theory is that many of the old magical books are filled with misleading information to fool the amateur. The meat of any magical ritual is much simpler than most of the books would have us believe.

I'm giving you a ritual with all the surplus fat trimmed off. No bat's wings, no mandrake root, no boiling caldrons nor broomsticks – in fact, all you're going to need for this work is 30 minutes a day in a quiet place.

If you follow these instructions step-by-step for 28 days, there's no reason at all why you shouldn't find yourself $10 richer by magical means – with the ability to do it again as often as you please.

Sure I hear you: "if it's so good, why doesn't he do it himself a few times and retire to Hawaii?" Tell you a secret: I do it all the time, and it works for me. And I know several people who call me up at intervals to say: "hey Geof – it worked again."

You see, once you're confident that you can magic up cash as and when you need it, there's no pressure to accumulate it. Yes, it's possible to build up a fat bank balance by magic – but it's easier to call up cash on a 'supply and demand' basis.

Yet most people find it difficult to believe that the old magic really does work, reliably and consistently: which is why I'm inviting you to try this.

Your background, education, or intelligence has nothing to do with your success at magic. You're reading this page, so you've got the necessary mental equipment to follow the directions through to a successful end.

The very first thing to do is to spend the next few days teaching your body to relax, so that you can tune into the area we're going to use together.

Try it this way: Lie down on your bed. Loosen all tight clothing. Kick off your shoes. Take off your glasses if you wear them. Take off your watch. Turn off the TV and radio. Close your eyes.

Start repeating the words "RELAX. UNWIND" in your mind, time after time. Use that phrase to shut out any other thoughts about when you're going to pay the rent, what you're going to have for supper and any other worries.

Sure enough, extra thoughts will start to creep into your mind. Throw them out with a mental shout of "RELAX. UNWIND."

Pick a convenient time to do that for 15 minutes each day – every day. Start on it as soon as possible, and schedule it regularly for at least five days – preferably a week. After that you can go on to the next step.

Once you've spent a few days relaxing regularly on your bed each day, make one change in the exercise. Start relaxing on a chair – an ordinary kitchen chair – instead. Why? Because as you learn to relax deeper and deeper, you're going to fall asleep if you're flat on your bed. That will do you good, but it won't get you any closer to the results we're trying for.

If you drop off to sleep on a chair, you'll fall off it. So you can pick yourself up and carry on with the exercise.

Once you're getting the hang of the relaxing, start this simple breathing exercise. Three minutes is long enough for this as you sit on the chair.

NOTE: If you suffer with a heart condition or any disorder which makes breathing dangerous for you, disregard this part of the exercise. <u>Check with your doctor if you are in any doubt.</u>

Deep breathing for someone who hasn't been doing it all their lives can cause dizziness, tingling in the arms and legs, and sundry other undesirable side effects.

So take it easy to start. Empty your lungs a little more than usual as you breathe out, but on no account push the last wisps of air out so that you feel pain in your stomach. If you feel any strain during this exercise, you're doing it wrong.

Breathe in, through your nose, counting 1-2-3-4 as you do it. Adjust the speed of the count so that your lungs are full, without strain, at the count of 4. Hold your breath for a count of 1-2. If you've filled up too much, you'll be tempted to close your throat to hold the air. Don't do that – it can cause physical problems. Just tense your stomach muscles slightly, and hold the air suspended in your lungs.

You should be able to tap yourself on the chest as you're holding your breath, and feel a puff of air leave your nose. That's not a part of the exercise – just an initial check to see if you're doing it right.

Now breathe out on the same slow count of 4. When your lungs feel empty, hold them like that for another count of 1-2.

Repeat that sequence a few times. Build it up by a couple of extra breaths a day, but stop doing it any time you feel dizziness creeping over you, or if spots of black and white start to dance at the corners of your vision.

As you practice, you'll find that your lung capacity will gradually increase. The result is improved relaxation because of the increase in your blood.

Now we're getting close to the beginning of the actual magic working. Your body is relaxing, bringing your mind closer to the Cosmic Ocean of energy which is waiting to serve you in your desires.

If you know about things called 'chakras', you can skip the next bit of explanation. If you don't, just accept this, read the words and let your inner mind absorb them.

You have many centers of power in your body which are connected directly with the Inner Planes – these are your chakras. Five of them are the most important to us at this time, and they exist on top of your head, in your throat, in your abdomen, around your genitals, and at your feet.

We're going to wake up those chakras by thinking about them. That will be sufficient for what we are doing – leave the greater awakening of the chakras to the advanced Yoga adepts.

Relax in your chair, and go into your breathing routine. I'll assume you've been doing it for several days, and your breath is moving deeply, naturally, in and out of your lungs.

After three minutes, pretend that a ball of brilliant white light is hanging above your head, just as if someone had placed a white, bright toy balloon up there.

As you do that bit of mind work, say this first Word of Power out loud: the word is "EH-HEH-YEH." All the E's are short, as you pronounce the vowel in the word 'Ten'. I've spelt out each Word of Power so that you say it just the way I've written it. The original Hebrew sounds approximately the way they're written here.

VcToria Comments: I pronounce this word AY HAY YAY. I found the 'e' in 'ten' a little confusing.

That particular word won't call up any devils for you. These three sounds are one way of pronouncing an ancient name for God.

Practice that part of the ritual each day for 15 minutes, and you'll begin to feel the first effects. Once you can firmly imagine that ball of light above your head, you'll feel a tingling sensation in your body, and a surge of energy running through you.

When you can sit down and firmly imagine that first ball of light above your head, carry the exercise a step further. Imagine that a band of light is moving downwards from the light above your head. The light moves down through your skull, and you should then pretend that it is expanding into a second ball of light under your chin, centered on your throat.

As you imagine that second surge of light, say the next Word of Power: "YEH-HO-VO-EL-OH-HEEM."

Again, after a while, you'll begin to feel a sensation of warmth and energy running through your neck and throat.

So your daily practice consists of a few minutes relaxing, breathing and them calling up those two balls of light.

After about a week, extend this mental exercise by pretending that the band of light is shining down through your body, growing into a third ball of light in your solar plexus. As it grows, say the Word of Power: "YEH-HO-VO-EL-OH-AH-VAY-DAH-ASS."

Now extend the band of light down to your genitals and imagine a fourth ball of light expanding there, at the same time saying: "SHAH-DIE-EL-KAY."

Lastly, send the shaft of light to your feet, and imagine yourself standing on a brilliant ball of light, as you say: "AH-DOH-NIGH-HA-AH-RETZ."

Lit up like a beacon in your mind, you're now ready to begin the magic working proper. Select a day to start, and give yourself 15 minutes each morning and evening to spend on your magic.

Decide that you will keep it up every day without interruption for 28 days – unless, of course, your $10-bill appears earlier than that.

Sit down, relax, and begin the breathing exercise. As you do it, feel your body becoming relaxed and heavy. When you feel totally limp, go through the balls of light imagining from your head to your feet, saying the five Words of Power at the appropriate times. You'll then be thoroughly charged up with mental power, and your next job is to get that power to move around you.

Think about the ball of light above your head. Then, as you are breathing out, pretend that a broad waterfall of white light is flowing out of the ball, cascading down the left side of your body. Imagine this flow being absorbed by the ball of light at your feet.

Then, as you start your next inhalation, pretend that the current light is sweeping up the right side of your body until it reaches the ball of brilliance at the top again.

Repeat that six times and you'll begin to feel the effects. A tingling will begin in your skin, and your relaxation will become even deeper.

Once that imagined flow of light is going well, round and round as you breathe in and out, start a second flow in a similar way. As you breathe out, pretend that the light is flowing down your body in front of you, rippling and cascading down your body until it reaches the lowest ball of light. Then imagine it flowing up your back to the top ball of light as you inhale.

Do that second imagined flow another six times. You will then be fully charged with the type of energy which can bring you material things – provided you direct that energy.

You're looking to bring yourself a $10 bill, so you now need to tune in to the color of money. Naturally the color associated with money is gold.

So, as you sit relaxed, feeling the white light flowing around you in the quiet of your imagination, you should pretend that the whiteness is gradually turning to a bright gold color.

Spend 15 minutes each morning and evening practicing that flow of golden light, and add one last thing to that twice-daily exercise.

As you get the golden light flowing around you, dip into your memory and recall what a $10 bill feels and looks like. Picture it in your mind, and pretend as hard as you can that a new $10 bill has appeared in your wallet or purse.

On no account try to calculate logically how it's going to arrive. Leave that job to the energy which you've created in your exercise. Your only task is to pretend that the money is in your hand. Recall how that bill feels, how it smells. Remember the way the paper crackles as you crumple it between your fingers. Think about the figures and patterns on a bill, and visualize the colors.

And that's all there is to it. Keep up your exercises twice a day until the money arrives. You've given yourself 28 days for this minor miracle to happen. The money may appear as a gift, or perhaps as a long forgotten loan being repaid. Maybe you'll find it in the street.

Somewhere, because of your ritual, coincidence and fate are working together to put an unexpected

10 bucks in your pocket. And when you've managed to do it once, you're all set to aim for bigger targets. There's no limit to what you can bring yourself by this method.

But begin slowly. Once you've done it to bring you a small sum of money, you'll gain the confidence to try for a larger sum. Then, if you wish, you can go on to a car, a house – anything you desire.

I'm quite sure it works. I personally know several people who use that ritual whenever they have bills to pay, or they need something. Whether it works for you consistently – or at all – is in the lap of the Gods of Chance and Coincidence, if there are such things.

I wish you the greatest of good fortune in your seeking.

Geof Gray-Cobb

Appendix

Several readers of the original column queried the meanings of the Words of Power. They are simply the names of the Cosmic Beings you call to assist you with the Work. They have no more 'meaning' than names like Smith, Cohen or McTavish.

You are calling on:

- Eh-Heh-Yeh – Jehovah [of the old Testament]
- Yeh-Ho-Vo-El-Oh-Heem – Jehovah, the Supreme.
- Yeh-Ho-Vo-El-Oh-Vay-Dah-Ass – Jehovah the Life-Giver
- Shah-Die-El-Kay – The Mighty One, the Source
- Ah-Doh-Nigh-Ha-Ah-Retz – Adonai, the Lamp unto my Feet.

None of them, to my knowledge, has ever been associated with Lucifer, unless it was before His Satanic Majesty was expelled from Heaven.

Note that the Power you call Them to use on your behalf is neutral, neither good nor bad. The end result depends entirely on your motives, imagination and personal aims in life.

CHAPTER 10

GAMBLING

Sun Sign: Leo, Aries and if it involves picking numbers then Pisces.

Moon Sign: Use under the Sun sign. Pisces, Cancer, Sagittarius.

Taken from *The Mystic Grimoire of Mighty Spells and Rituals* by Frater Malak AKA Geof Gray-Cobb

THE TERRIFIC WIN-IT-ALL SPELL

This Spell needs a private place to set the luck vibrations going your way before you join a game or make a bet. It's designed to turn luck vibrations your way in contests where chance is the chief factor in winning.

Make sure you're alone and unseen by others.

If possible, perform this Spell during the day. Facing toward the sun, throw your hands and arms upward and outward, fingers straight and palms forward. Move your feet about 24 inches apart, so that you're standing in the shape of an X.

If it's after dark, face west if you are performing the spell before midnight and east after midnight.

GAMBLING

Say, (or think if you maybe overheard):

> "Sun! Sun! The power that be,
> "The Gods of Chance shall smile on me,
> "While Lady Luck shall steal away
> "The fortune from my rival's play."

Lower your arms to your side, keep your eyes closed and touch your money, turning it over in your pocket or purse. Turn around three times to the right, stamp your right foot three times and open your eyes. Go about and place your bets or buy the lottery tickets.

CHAPTER 11

BUSINESS

Sun Sign: Aries, Leo, Capricorn, Aquarius

Moon Sign: Under the Sun signs when the Moon is in Taurus or Capricorn

If your business relates to opening anything travel related (e.g., agent or a book store) you may add Gemini to both the Sun Sign and the Moon sign.

Once you have decided on the business and have the ground work done you need to decide on what type of opening you wish to have. Either way once you have decided we need to set the stage for growth.

Prior to the opening you have chosen a name. I always recommend the name to be vibrating to a three. Many folks will be advised from a numerologist to name it to a vibration of an eight. They are wrong. Why? An eight attracts harvest, BUT if you are making your daily income by having to be annoyed all the time, then is it worth it? The eight does not recognize anything except material.

Now if you name your company with a vibration of a three it will attract creativity, people with like-minded desires towards you and basically three means that it is attractive in a creative manner to all folks.

I named my company The Alternative Universe. It vibrates to a three. Now interestingly enough AU is also the symbol for gold. I opened this company in 1998. To this day [2020] I have had a very creative, busy and substantial company that just keeps growing in creative ways. I let go of things as they died out either in desire or no longer the rage (e.g., in 2001 I taught Tarot cards, etc). The internet was not as it is today. However, as the internet grew and people started to study from there, the classes no longer filled. I stopped teaching and moved to another area. The vibration of three does this for you.

Now that you know how to name your business, you can also use the pendulum to ask if it is the correct name. Choose quite a few and you will come up with the one that vibrates for you.

Now under the suggested Sun signs and Taurus or Capricorn Moon energies we set the opening spell for the magic of wealth and joy to enter into your life.

Move to your place of magical working or altar. Find your Group Leader Card and the other four. By now you should have them situated on your altar or the special place you have chosen to keep them. Choose the Angels that represent the day, month, date, zodiac sign and time of the exact opening. Lay them in a circle on your altar or working place. Take the name of your business and type it out and print. Or, if you have business cards use one of them. Take the company name and place it inside the circle. Again you will have two Group Leader cards. Take your Personal Group Leader card and stand it up. If you have the pyramid, stand it against the North side. Place your business name beside your Personal Group Leader card.

Sit in the chair of relaxation in front of the altar. Close your eyes and ask that the names of the Angels that you have placed before you enter into the realm of energy that you are producing.

Envision your company being busy. Now what is that going to take? Do you need the public to be your income? Then see this as it happens. However, in between your visual pictures stop and ask in your mind 'is this the correct scene'? You will hear a resounding 'yes' or 'no'. If it is 'yes' continue with your setting up the future of desire with the seeds you are seeding into your subconscious. If you hear 'no' then you need to stop and re-evaluate. If you are only focusing on the money then that is why. Go back in and focus upon the joy that you will feel as the actions of the company build.

When you are done do not forget to thank the Angels and say ETA MESA EST to allow them to leave.

You may do this programming of success for your business as many times as you like as the opening day arrives. If I was doing an opening of business I would do this once a day for the seven days prior to the opening.

THE INSTANT BUSINESS-SUCCESS SPELL

Taken from *The Mystic Grimoire of Mighty Spells and Rituals* by Frater Malak AKA Geof Gray-Cobb

Take three single cents and wrap them in a cloth.

Say:

> "Money, money let us see
> "Your powers flow from you to me."

Place the coins on a table and extend your writing hand above them, fingers together, palm down. Close your eyes and then point the forefinger of the same hand and write a large dollar sign three times in the air in front of you.

Say:

> "Golden showers, see them clear,
> "They grow and never disappear."

Open your eyes and unwrap the coins, saying:

> "These cents shall symbolize for me
> "A growing trade. So shall it be."

Mount the three coins on a triangular piece of cardboard or wood, and place them unobtrusively near your desk or cash drawer.

Never draw attention to them, but if someone asks what they are, you may say: "They're my good luck pieces."

CHAPTER 12

LEGAL

Sun sign: Naturally having the perfect time to have a court case may be out of your control but if it is not, choose to have it under the sign of Libra.

Moon sign: Libra and Capricorn

Taken from The Mystic Grimoire of Mighty Spells and Rituals by Frater Malak AKA Geof Gray-Cobb

THE FANTASTIC WIN-AT-LAW SPELL

Perform this Spell at midnight before any Court appearance.

Place the papers associated with your legal battle on a table. Place a candle to the right of them. Exactly at midnight light the candle. Sit at the table and as the candle burns brightly, study the flame closely.

When it is burning clearly and steadily, stare into the flame. Lay your writing hand on the papers and think about whatever result you are hoping for.

Then say:

> "Rash of Mithra hear me!
> "My cause is right and true,
> "Influence the powers that judge,
> "I ask this boon of you."

Stand up and walk three times around your chair, to the right. Sit down again, lay your hand on the papers and stare into the candle flame. The flame will be moving now: sit still until it steadies. Say:

> "Rash of Mithra, I thank Thee for Thy aid against ....[name your opponents].

Extinguish the candle, turn on the lights and before the candle cools, carefully pour a little of the liquid wax onto a piece of plain paper. Fold the paper and let it cool before putting it under your pillow for the night.

In the morning write the name 'RASH OF MITHRA' on the paper and keep it with you during the day. Keep it out of sight, however, and destroy it after your law case is settled.

INCANTATION TO WIN A LEGAL ACTION

Taken from *NAP: The Miracle of New Avatar Power* by Geof Gray-Cobb

1. Mighty Ielahiah* who holds sway over the decisions of men; Thou shalt bring Thy power to bear on my behalf in the legal action which is pending.

2. I command that I shall be successful in this, my hour of need. Thou hast the ability to aid me in achieving this desire. Hear the Word and be obedient to It and me: NAB-RAT-AGLA-SURE-AN-AT. So mote it be.

* Pronounced EYE-EEL-AH-HE-YAH.

CHAPTER 13

TRAVEL

Sun Sign: Aries, Leo, Sagittarius, Aquarius, Gemini.

Moon Sign: To be used under the Sun signs. Virgo, Aries, Capricorn and Libra.

If you are traveling to specifically do a spiritual journey, the Sun sign should be Pisces and Moon sign in Pisces whilst you are there.

Taken from *The Mystic Grimoire of Mighty Spells and Rituals* by Frater Malak AKA Geof Gray-Cobb

THE BRILLIANT TRAVEL-SAFETY SPELL

This is another simple Spell which brings powerful protective influences to you.
To ensure a safe journey or to turn malignant travel influences to less harmful ones.

Say [or think] three times:

"Susabo, stay with me on my journey."

Pronounce His Name "Soo-Sah-Bo" with the emphasis on the second syllable.
If, while invoking this protection, you are holding a piece of blue cloth or paper, you will reinforce the protection.

CHAPTER 14

ASTRAL TRAVEL

Sun Sign: Aquarius is the best but we can use any Sun sign as long as you use the Moon energy as advised.

Moon Sign: Aquarius, Sagittarius, Pisces, Cancer.

ASTRAL TRAVEL

In 1973 Geof must have decided that he would start to do a series of psychic work. He chose Astral Travel for his first choice. As I have promised I have added all of the works that I have not re-published in book form and created them in this encyclopedia. His book *The Miracle of New Avatar Power* was written and sold over 100,000 copies that then took his life in another direction. Therefore it appears no other editions of the series were written.

I have only been able to astral travel in the physical form of being awake once. This was also unintended. I was sitting at my dining room table in 1995. I suppose I was daydreaming. All of a sudden the energy of my physical body, call it the soul, zoomed out of my head and I was in this box above myself. In this box was my brother who had passed in 1971.

In 1971 he was hit whilst on the back of a motorcycle. Helmets were not the law back then and he landed on his head. He sustained so much brain damage that at the hospital they had him hooked up to tubes to breathe. My parents chose to let him go.

There he was in this box on a motorcycle going in a circle. This took all but a few seconds. Mental telepathy is how I would describe this. I knew it was him. I knew he was my spirit guide. However, I was so shocked that I banged back into my body with a massive jolt. From that day forth I always referred to my brother, who was named Jeremy in this life, as my guide. I called upon him in times of anguish. I am sure he helped me to get where I am today. The motorcycle I feel was simply a prop to enhance the recognition.

Now that is the one and only time I have been able to do this, and as I said it was not intentional. What I learnt from that is you have to stop your mind from thinking. A feat in itself.

I also question others who claim to be able to do so. Why? First and foremost if I was able to attain this ability all the time, at will, the first thing I would do would be to visit Area 51, take notes mentally and write a book on it in such accuracy that it would be impossible for anyone not to know that astral travel can be done at will. No one has done this and therefore I question it. I am not saying it is impossible, but I would love for anyone who claims to be able to do this to enter into my home and then e-mail me with 100% accuracy all of that which I am doing at a particular time and day.

However, having said this, and having had that experience I do plan to take next year, as I will not be busy in the winter, and practice this unique way of manoeuvring energy.

CHAPTER 15

ASTRAL TRAVEL BOOK
by Geof Gray-Cobb

This chapter is a duplication of the first booklet by Geof Gray-Cobb in an intended series of short manuscripts offering practical methods of mastering the psychic sciences

BIOGRAPHICAL SKETCH

The author, Geof Gray-Cobb [August 15th, 1928 – May 12th, 2009] was an experienced practitioner of the occult.

He researched the paranormal for over 20 years [by 1973] and had studied phenomena, divination, witchcraft, ritual magic and other allied subjects in the U.S, Canada, England, South Africa and the Middle East.

He held a degree in Metaphysics, and was a graduate of Mind Development Inc. conscious awareness techniques, and was also a graduate of the Duval School of Hypnotism.

He was vice-president of the Hermetic Order of Campo Santo, a non-profit fraternal organization dedicated to teaching self-help by spiritual and occult means.

INTRODUCTION

Would you like to fly on the winds of space, roam the corridors of the galaxy, travel invisibly from here to anywhere, and feel the supreme release from all earthly bondage?

That, in part, describes astral travel. This section of the encyclopedia offers you the way to achieve it.

Books on astral travel – or astral projection – can be found in every store that deals with the occult.

The experiences of successful astral projections have been recorded and repeated in books, magazines and newspapers ever since the Out-Of-The-Body-Experience [OOBE] was recognized.

This section takes a different approach. Very few case histories are included. What you are offered here is a practical method which will enable you to master the art of astral projection – a complete primer for the beginner.

Mental and physical exercises are included, plus suggestions on environment, diet, times and when you are most likely to achieve a successful astral journey.

If you follow this step-by step course, you can astrally project, safely and with reasonable ease.

Methods of alleged 'instant' astral travel exist, but I have found that, like instant coffee, the results lack the body, flavor and stimulation of the genuine article.

For total satisfaction, I contend that there is nothing – yet – to beat the steady mastering of the art over a period of time.

Astral travel can be mastered, by anyone. I do not promise you will astrally project today, nor even tomorrow. But the methods laid out for you here have worked for many people: with a minimal dedication and half-an-hour per day of your time, you too, can learn the art.

WHAT IS ASTRAL PROJECTION

Mystics have long stated – and science is beginning to agree – that each of us consists of more than a fleshy body and bony skeleton housing a mind and brain. The metaphysical concept is that our physical body is interpenetrated by an astral body, just as a sponge holds water. The astral body is formed of matter which is thinner and more tenuous than smoke, and can, by an act of will, be released from its home in the physical body to roam free, taking with it the five physical senses. Some people consider the astral body to be part of the soul which leaves the body at death.

The concept of the soul has been argued by theologians, atheists, agnostics, mystics, scientists and laymen for centuries. Generally, the only point of agreement they have reached is that a dead person is somehow 'different' from that person when he or she was alive. That 'difference' can be called the soul.

'Something', at death, goes from the body, and that something was what made the body move and live.

Astral projection is the art and discipline which enables anyone to move part of the 'something' out of his or her body at will.

Then when that part, which we call the astral body, is free of the physical body, the sense of sight, hearing, touch, taste and smell go along with it.

HOW IS ASTRAL TRAVEL PERFORMED

You lie down on a bed or couch, close your eyes, and apply the methods described in this section.

Soon, a floating sensation occurs, and you feel yourself drifting up out of your body, or moving across the room. On the bed your physical body lies as if in a deep sleep, breathing and functioning perfectly – but your center of awareness, your astral body, has moved away.

When you are in your astral body, you can turn around and look at your physical body lying motionless on the bed. Then when you are tired of drifting around your room, or around your home, you can – with the speed of thought – zip off to anywhere in the Universe.

With practice, you can overhear conversations in distant places, or watch events happening thousands of miles away, as if you were a flesh-and-blood spectator. You can do everything, which you can do in your physical body – except one. You cannot move physical objects.[1]

You can float through anything, as if you were thinner than the thinnest mist, and you can soar like a bird far above the earth, looking down on the towns and cities below you.

Your astral body does not breathe air, so you can explore the deepest ocean or fly to the top of the highest mountain – or to the Moon, if that is what you wish.

Astral travel is one of the most exhilarating experiences, and it lays the foundation for many other occult abilities provided it is learned thoroughly.

IS IT DIFFICULT TO ASTRAL TRAVEL?

Astral journeys are simple once you have mastered the knack. It takes time, just as learning any new

---

[1] A few references can be found to people who say that they have moved physical objects while astral traveling. That seems to be a particular application of mind called 'Psychokinesis,' and is rare.

ability does, but once you have acquired the ability to drift out of your body in full, conscious flight you will understand the glorious freedoms which await you.

And after you have explored the physical universe in your astral body, there is the whole of the Astral Plane to be discovered. There you can build or create anything by the power of your thought, and you can arrange matters so that your astral creations gradually become realities in the physical world. That is true magic, and will form the basis of another book in this series.

First, make your astral body your willing servant. Later, you can work your miracles.

VcToria Comments: As noted above, no more of these series were created. However, you can now see that Dad wanted you to learn this profound action so that magic would be easy and access to the energy shifts would be simple. I am going to make next year [2021] my intention to truly do a daily programming of this section of the book.

OUTLINE OF THE METHOD

Learning to astral travel takes place in a number of well-defined steps. Physical relaxation, memory, recall, visualization and the desire to travel form a large part of the initial work.

The exercises which will train you to astral travel will take no more than 30 minutes a day.

Regular practice – just as if you were training your physical body – is vital to success.

If you follow these instructions, in the order given, there is every hope that you will be conducting conscious astral journeys to wherever you wish to go within 30 days.

The first important key is physical relaxation. You will achieve this by feeding your mind key phrases which will begin to work automatically to let the tensions float out of every muscle of your body.

While you are doing that you will spend a little time convincing yourself that astral travel is possible.

However much you wish to astral travel, your early training, conditioning and personal beliefs may have planted firm biases deep in your mind.

One of these biases may be that the concept of separating of yourself from your physical body is ludicrous in the extreme.

You may sincerely want to believe that your physical body can stay laid out on a bed, while part of you – your astral body – roams the world. But somewhere inside of you a nagging doubt may exist, which denies that astral travel, or that the astral body, can possibly exist.

Like mastering any other ability, you will master astral travel much more quickly when you believe with every level of your being that astral travel is possible.

If I may draw a parallel, there was a time in the athletic world when everyone believed that running a four minute mile was impossible.

The time for the mile was regularly clipped each year by a second or two, but the four minute mile was a barrier which defied the best efforts of the fittest and fastest runners.

The magic time of four minutes seemed to be impregnable for nine solid years. Gunder Haegg, a Swede, came closet, running the mile in 4 minutes 1.4 seconds.

After Haegg managed to get that close, in 1945, no-one got closer to the magic barrier for nearly a decade.

Then, in May, 1954, an English athlete, Roger Bannister, ran the mile in 3 minutes 59.4 seconds. The Mystic fence had been hurdled!

Promptly, athlete after athlete achieved a four-minute mile, and now the world record is almost 9 seconds under the time which once was thought to be impossible to beat.

Can you understand the concept? Once athletes knew that four minute miles could be beaten, it removed some sort of mental block, and soon afterwards, the four-minute mile became old hat.

It's much the same with astral travel. Once you know it is possible, it removes the last doubt from your mind and you just go ahead and do it.

Probably the chief mental block to astral travel is convincing yourself that you too can split into two parts – a physical and an astral body.

Seeing is believing, so we practice a simple exercise which enables you to see your astral body, or a part of it, separating your physical body.

Once you have seen this separation it opens up your 'belief channels' and most doubts of your ability to astral travel promptly vanish into thin air.

Having reached that stage, the work begins in real earnest. You begin what I have called the 'cue' travel. This is an intermediate step towards astral travel, and as you practice it, you will find that you slip imperceptibly into astral traveling.

It's difficult, in fact, to decide where the dividing line exists. Cue travel is easy to explain, easy to carry out, and as you practice it and slip deeper into the correct frame of mind you will suddenly realize one day that what started as a cue journey has turned into an astral journey.

I have found this to be a valid road towards astral traveling, simply because it effectively by-passes the extreme challenge of explaining what astral travel feels like, and exactly how you get there.

Without having to understand complicated explanations on the what, where and why of astral travel, you find yourself actually experiencing astral travel, which is far better than any words you can read on a page.

And before we proceed any further, a word of warning. You should recognize that one of the quickest ways to slow your progress in any form of occult ability is to strain and strive for that ability.

Clenched teeth, knitted brows, knotted fists and sheer dogged determination will get you exactly no place towards astral traveling.

On the other hand, cue traveling, by giving your mind a path to follow, leads inevitably to astral travel. No stress, no strain, and you slip into an astral journey as effortlessly as you drop asleep when you are dead tired.

Once you have traveled astrally a few times you'll recognize the mental state you need to reach for 'lift off'. After that it's only a matter of extending your journeys by regular practice.

PREPARATIONS FOR ASTRAL TRAVEL

These preparations are intended for the beginner of astral travel. When you are adept at it, many of these requirements fall away. The idea here is to set up the most favorable conditions for the first vital steps.

SURROUNDINGS

Until you are really practiced at the art of astral journeying, a quiet environment will give you the best chance of success.

While you are 'out' traveling, any disturbance of your physical body will bring you zapping back as quickly as thought. Apart from being startling, you can also give yourself a mild headache by coming back too abruptly.

So arrange a time and place where you can lie on a couch or bed, in a dim light, undisturbed for about 30 minutes.

Switch off the radio, the TV and turn all phones to off. Hope that no one comes calling to bang on the door or ring your front door bell.

Steady background noise is no problem. If you live near a freeway for instance, and normally sleep through traffic noises, you'll have no problem with astral traveling. Sudden disturbances are what you need to try and avoid.

The room should be dim. Heavy drapes or a blanket pinned at the window should cut the light down to a level where it's difficult to read the small print of a newspaper.

On the other hand, a small amount of light, such as a very dim night-light, is useful so that when you come back from your journey you can easily orient yourself. Coming back to a totally pitch black room from an astral journey can leave you wondering which way is up, and where you are for a while.

YOUR PHYSICAL BODY

Some disturbances which interrupt a potential astral journey can come from outside, while others can be self-generated.

Aches, pains and discomfort are a decided impediment to the first steps of astral travel. So I suggest you do not try to move out of your body immediately after a heavy meal, – a touch of indigestion or flatulence will put a brake on your progress.

The ideal is to be able to lie down so comfortably that you can almost forget that you have a physical body. In that state, astral separation happens easily. If you have a headache, or you're tense from the day's hustle and bustle, or something is worrying you, practice the relaxation which is described in the next section until your body is limp and detached.

Generally speaking, during your first attempts, you will find that eating heavy, stodgy foods before an astral journey will obstruct your progress, while a light meal of fresh fruit and vegetables will assist you. You probably should not go to the other extreme and starve yourself for hours before you travel.

Experiment in this area. Some people 'fly' better on an empty stomach, others prefer some food inside them. As far as tobacco and alcohol are concerned, most people find them both to impede astral journeys. Smoking just before traveling seems to dull the clarity of the experience, while alcohol taken before the trip is likely to make you lose control of your journeying.

Uncontrolled astral travel is simple – we all do some of that every night when we sleep and dream. What we are aiming for here is total control over your destinations and, later, your astral environment.

BEST TIMES TO TRAVEL

Again you need to experiment. Many people find that they travel most easily and most accurately between 10 pm and midnight. Others find that mid-afternoon is good, while a few people swear that 5 am is their best time.

One factor you can check out is the phase of the Moon. Probably 75% of astral travelers achieve their greatest success during the seven days midway between the New Moon and Full Moon.

Look up the date of the New Moon in an almanac, wait three or four days, then begin your first attempts at true, controlled astral travel.

VcToria Comments: Nowadays you can Google the dates of the Moon or know that while I am in the physical world, I post a monthly section on my website and in my monthly newsletter that gives you these times. You can sign up for my newsletter at www.alternativeuniverse.ca

SUMMARY OF PREPARATIONS

You will realize that I have been suggesting conditions which are as ideal as possible to give you maximum chance of success.

Later, you will be able to astral travel in broad daylight while an electric storm is raging, but before you reach that happy state, you need to make your first astral journey.

The first trip is the important one. Once you've accomplished it, you will finally know that you can do it, and the last impeding shreds of doubt will be banished forever.

Conversely, if you are careless with your first preparations, you may be setting yourself up for a first-time failure. That is not good, for your doubts about the practicability of astral travel will doubly reinforce, and may take longer to subdue.

Some people take to astral travel as easily as a bird takes to air. Others labor for weeks before they feel the exciting tremors of their astral body drifting loose from the physical body.

You are an individual, and the instructions in this section represent guide lines, not hard and fast rules.

Let your intuition be your guide. If a suggestion of mine feels 'wrong' to you, then change it. Experiment with your environment, state of mind and physical status.

These suggestions suit the majority of people. You may be the one who is not in the majority. So bend these guide-lines, and reverse them totally if you wish.

As a rule, if you instinctively feel that you have a better method of achieving any part of the described conditions, then try your method. In astral travel, and also in all occult matters, you should let your hunches and your conscience be your guide.

I assure you that if you sincerely wish to astral travel, then you will astral travel, no matter what.

RELAXATION

You can practice this method of physical relaxation at any time, but you should always precede any astral journey with at least five minutes of these exercises.[2]

Lay yourself full length on your bed or couch, flat on your back. All clothing should be loose and your feet should be bare. You can relax [and astral travel] in pajamas, nightgown, your best suit or in a state of nature, but you must be comfortable, and all straps, belts and elastics should be removed.

Take off your wrist watch if you wear one and put it somewhere well away from the bed. At one stage during relaxation your hearing may become much

---

[2] If you have mastered any other method of relaxation which works well for you then use that method instead of this one.

more acute, and the racket of a watch suddenly clacking away a few feet from your ear can be distracting.

Do not cross your legs. Your feet should be an inch or two apart. Let your arms rest beside your body, wherever they are comfortable. If you cannot find a position for them which feels right, try laying your hands one on top of each other on your chest or stomach.

If you feel you need a pillow under your head, make it a thin one. If your head is bent forward it will restrict your breathing.

Once you are settled in a comfortable position on your back, close your eyes. Just let them shut gently.

Now breathe in deeply.

> **NOTE:** IF YOU HAVE A HEART CONDITION, OR SUSPECT YOU MAY HAVE ONE, OMIT THE DEEP BREATHING DESCRIBED HERE. THE SAFEST COURSE WOULD BE TO CHECK WITH YOUR DOCTOR.

Fill your lungs full, but not so filled that they feel strained or bursting. Reverse the air flow and exhale slowly, letting the air out of your lungs a little more than usual. Again, do not thrust every last ounce of air out of your chest by sheer muscular tension.

Breathe in again, deeply and slowly, at the same time whispering a long-drawn-out: "REE-E-E-EE". Then as you breathe out, whisper "LAX", extending the syllable so that you reach the whole 'X' sound as your lungs are just comfortably empty.

Continue to do this about 10 times. Don't bother to count – 8 times or 12 times will do just as well.

As you are breathing and repeating the drawn-out "RE–LAX", think about your whole body. Run your attention from the top of your scalp to the soles of your feet.

As you do this you will feel a heaviness creeping through your legs, arms, trunk and head.

Let your breathing subside to its normal flow, but continue to repeat 'RE–LAX' in time with the rise and fall of your chest. Keep that up for at least five minutes.

Then stop whispering 'Relax' and proceed to whatever next step you have reached in your astral travel program – either seeing your astral body, physical cue travel, mental cue travel or astral travel itself.

SEEING YOUR ASTRAL BODY

By seeing your astral body – or part of it – you will remove any doubt about the reality of the situation. Once you know your astral body can be seen separately from your physical body, you have taken a large psychological step towards full astral travel.

HAND SEEING

Climb quietly and limply from your relaxation couch. Switch on a dim light – again experiment with how much illumination you need – and sit down so that you are facing a blank light-colored wall.

Arrange a table in front of you and rest your elbows on it, putting your hands flat together in an attitude of prayer, with your thumbs about 12 inches from your face.

Now move your hands about half–an–inch apart. Look through the space between your hands at the wall beyond them. You will promptly see about three hands as your eyes focus on the wall.

Shift your hands, maintaining them a half-inch apart, until you can look between them at the wall with one eye – although you must keep both eyes open.

If that seems confusing, temporarily shut one eye and move your hands until you can look straight through the space between your palms. Then keeping your hands and head stationary, open the closed eye.

After sitting in this position for a minute or so, you will feel a prickly sensation in your hands, or a warmth in your palms. Breathe a little more deeply and regularly than normal – but do not overdo it.

Watch for a brighter line of light to appear around the outline of your palms as you look. Let your eyes blink normally as you sit relaxed, peeping through your hands. On no account stare, squint or screw up your eyes.

You will suddenly realize that part of the space between your palms seems to be filled with mist. This is your astral body, or rather, a portion of it. View it for a couple of minutes, watching it swirl and shift, and then terminate the exercise.

If, after five minutes of calm examination, you have not seen the Gray mist, or any other change between your palms, alter the intensity of the lighting. Try moving the light source to other parts of the room. You may find that if the light is in your field of vision it impedes the phenomenon, so sit with your back to the light.

With patience and experimentation, you'll succeed, and once you have the knack of it, you'll be able to see your astral body after a very short time of looking for it.

This test, apart from setting up basic positive belief patterns in your mind, is also most useful for assessing your progress.

You will discover that the quicker you see this smoky emanation from your hands, the 'looser' your astral body is inside your physical body.

If you see the Gray mist very shortly after sitting down, this shows, mentally and physically, you are in excellent shape for an astral journey. Conversely, if the mist takes a long while to appear, you probably need to work on relaxation for a while longer before attempting astral flight.

SEEING THE COMPLETE ETHERIC BODY

You may have heard of the human aura. This is an area of psychic force which extends two or three feet all around your physical body.

Clairvoyants and psychics can see this field of force as a shimmering colored envelope surrounding the body.

Part of the aura is known as the 'etheric', and your etheric is also part of your astral body. It is, in fact, the thing you have been viewing between your hands during the preceding exercise.

The etheric usually stays close to the surface of the skin, and under the right conditions you can see it, enveloping your body like a close-fitting garment.

Seeing your complete etheric is an even better exercise towards mastering astral travel. Again, it sets up powerful belief patterns in the depths of your mind, and enables natural doubts and scepticism to be quelled.

The etheric is most easily seen when you are naked. In fact, it's probably easier to see someone else's etheric than it is to see your own.

The conditions required are much the same as for 'hand-seeing' – dim light and physical relaxation.

SEEING YOUR OWN ETHERIC

Strip completely, removing all jewelry, wrist watch, bobby pins, and other metal objects. If you wear glasses, remove them too, unless you are totally incapable of seeing without them. Contact lenses can be worn, however.

Stand a few feet in front of a full length mirror, having arranged the lighting so that it approximates to the level you found suitable for the 'hand seeing' experiment.

Now stick a circular piece of white paper, about the size of a dime, on the surface of the mirror in such a position that when you stand looking at your full-length reflection, the paper is seen in the middle of your forehead, about an inch above your eyes.

Finally, move all furniture away from where you are standing until you have a clear space of at least three feet all around you. If you have the space, six feet is even better.

With your arms hanging loose at your side and your feet about 12 inches apart, stand and look at the piece of paper on the mirror. Keep your eyes on the paper, but focus your attention on your reflection.

You will soon notice a Gray mist forming around your reflection. Raise your arms slightly and you will see the mist move with your arms.

You are seeing your etheric, part of your astral body. As you become more practiced at seeing it, you will notice that it expands and contracts as you breathe in and out. Also, notice that it is thicker around your hips, pelvis and head.

Later, you may begin to see colors shifting within the mist. That is extremely encouraging – you will have progressed from seeing your relatively dense etheric to the state of being able to see your aura, a much more tenuous and fine phenomenon.

The ability to see your aura shows that astral travel will probably come easily to you. It also indicates that your psychic awareness is strong – not only will you be able to fully explore the astral plane and its associated areas, you will also be able to expand your experience in almost any other area of the occult which interests you.

SEEING A PARTNER'S ETHERIC

Just as you can see your own etheric when you stand nude before a mirror, so you can, under the right conditions, see the etheric – or the aura – of anyone who is prepared to cooperate in the experiment.

A word of warning. This entails both of you being naked, under quiet and relaxed conditions, which may arouse sexual emotions.

Tension of any kind is a direct hindrance to cultivating the inner psychic powers needed to see the etheric or the aura. While sexual tensions are eminently useful in some advanced occult exercises, allied to Tantra and sex magic, they are more of a hindrance than a help in the early experiments and disciplines of astral travel.

Only if you can maintain a detached frame of mind when gazing at a nude body should you try this exercise.

You need a room where you can clear a space so that you may stand about six feet from your partner with enough empty space around you for the nearest piece of furniture to be at least three feet from either of you.

As before, a six feet clearance around you both is the ideal, but that would use an empty space roughly 18 feet x 12 feet, which is impractical unless you have a totally unfurnished room to use for the experiment.

This etheric-seeing exercise can also be carried out with great success in the open air, by the light of a full Moon, on a secluded beach or in a woodland clearing.

However, unless you can be absolutely certain of total privacy, there is a danger that concern about being spied upon may repress the necessary relaxed, detached state of mind which is necessary for success with this exercise.

Having found the necessary space, both participants should strip totally, removing all possible metallic objects outside the cleared area.

Unless outdoors, when you will have to make do with what Mother Nature provides, arrange the lighting so that it is dim and shadowless, and does not shine in the eyes of either person.

A low, wattage lamp on the floor, behind a solid piece of furniture and perhaps further shielded by cardboard screens, is likely to produce the right conditions.

Stand six feet apart, facing each other, feet slightly apart and arms hanging loosely at your side. Both should look at a point between the partner's eyes, without strain or tension.

Within two or three minutes, one or both of you should see the Grayish mist outlining the body of the other. At that stage you can begin to describe to each other what you see, comparing impressions. Notice that if one person takes a deep breath, the etheric – or the aura, if it is in view – grows in strength and apparent brightness.

Normally, females have brighter and more distinct etherics and auras than males. Thus the male of a male/female pair of experimenters is more likely to see the etheric, rather than vice versa.

PHYSICAL CUE TRAVEL

Having mastered the art of relaxation, and experimented with seeing your etheric, you are now physically and mentally prepared to move on to the practice of cue travel.

Cue travel begins by physically taking a short journey, on foot, through your home, picking up three identification points – or 'cues', hence the name – en route.

These identification points are printed in black-and-white on pages 109-113. For excellent occult reasons, you are going to complete these cues by coloring them.

VcToria comments: You may order these, all colored, on my web store on my website or color them yourself. I have, as I do to all the items needed to work any of my late Fathers books, inserted the magic energy needed to work them at their maximum potential under a Pisces Moon. See web store: www.alternativeuniverse.ca

Any occult tool which you make yourself has infinitely more power than anything created for you by another person – and these cues will be as much occult tools for you as any magic wand or robe is to a fully-fledged ritual magic-worker.

VcToria comments: In response to the above paragraph, energy nowadays is understood a lot more. Anything you order in regard to all of the books on magic have energy inserted into them under the Pisces Moon, therefore making them as powerful as if you had done the work yourself.

Doing it yourself: Scan the pages from this book. The square is to be colored yellow; the triangle will be red; and the circle will be blue. The colors should be as bright as possible – a good, deep sunny yellow, bright blood red, and a solid bright blue.

Alternatively, large felt-tip markers are ideal for coloring in the shapes of your cues, and some people have also tried 'Day-Glo' colors with success.

One way or another, color your three cues as brightly as possible in their respective colors. If you wish to be occultly 'correct' when you make these aids to astral travel, you should sit alone in a room at midnight within 24 hours of the full moon as you do your coloring.

Relax and enjoy their creation as you color them, to give them maximum power.

You now need to find places for your cues in your home.

As you stand up from the place where you intend to lie during astral journeys, you should be able to see the yellow square cue card across the room. Naturally, the best place to astral travel from is the same place where you have been practicing relaxation.

So, using a thumbtack or sticky tape, mount your yellow square cue on the wall at eye level where you can stand two feet from it and look at it.

Now decide which is the furthest point you can walk in your home from the yellow cue, without ascending or descending a flight of stairs. In a split-level, the few steps between levels do not count as a full flight.

If you live in one room, then the furthest point will be diagonally across the room from the yellow square. This second point is where you are going to mount your red triangle cue card, also at eye level, in a position where you can look at it from two feet away.

Having fixed your yellow square and red triangle cues, mount the blue circle card somewhere midway between the other two, at eye level as before.

All three cards should be well lit, so that you can see the colors easily as you stand before them. The yellow cue, in the same room that you relax in, should have its own switched lamp near it, so that you can relax in the dim and switch on the light when you begin the exercises.

The idea is that as you walk from one cue card to the next you make a tour of your room, apartment or house, starting and ending at your relaxation couch. Having placed your cards, make your first physical cue journey.

Lie down and relax as instructed. Gently and slowly slide your feet to the floor, stand up and walk to your viewing position, for Cue 1, the yellow square.

Stand about two feet from it and fix your eyes on the centre of the square for a full two minutes.

Allow your eyes to drift out of focus if you wish, so that you see a double square, but keep your attention riveted on the yellow square. After about a minute the square will seem to have a bright bluish edge drifting on and off it.

Keep your attention and your thoughts on the square until the two minutes are up.

Now look at a light-colored surface to the side of the square. You will see a blue square drifting in front of your eyes. Look at that blue square for about half-a-minute as it fades.

Now walk slowly and easily to Cue 2, the red triangle, and repeat the process. This time you will see a greenish–blue edge forming around the triangle as you look at it, and when you look away at the wall a green-blue triangle will hover before you. Its actual color will depend on what shade of red you have used.[3]

Now walk to Cue 3, the blue circle and stare at it for two minutes as you have done with the other two cues. The circular after-image you will see this time is yellow.

As the yellow circle fades, walk to your relaxation couch, lie down and close your eyes, relaxing for a minute or two.

You have carried out your first physical cue journey. Practice this daily for at least a week.

VcToria Comments: If you are color blind I suggest you purchase the cue cards from my web store as the colors will be correct.

MENTAL CUE TRAVEL

When you are well–practiced at physical cue travel, you are ready to proceed to mental cue travel. Mental cue travel will automatically lead to astral traveling. How long you have to do it depends on yourself, but regular mental cue travel will one day assuredly merge into a true astral journey for you.

Mental cue travel consists simply of carrying out a physical cue journey in your mind and memory. Your regular daily physical ritual of standing up, looking at the yellow cue card, then walking to the second and third before returning to your couch will by now be engraved on your memory. You will have

---

[3] Even if you are totally color blind, carry out the exercise as directed, watching the shapes form and drift in front of your eyes. You need not worry if you cannot detect the colors.

no trouble at all pretending that you are taking the physical journey when in fact you are lying on your couch.

Lie down and relax for five minutes, as usual. By this time your body will respond quickly to the thoughts of 'Relax'.

When you are fully heavy and limp, bring your mind to bear on the cue cards. Keep your eyes closed, pretend that you are moving off the bed, walking across the room and standing in front of the yellow cue card. Recall how it feels to be standing there, and how the yellow square shimmers and moves with its blue outline forming before your eyes. Then recall the floating blue after-image as it appears on the wall.

After two minutes or so, pretend that you are walking to the red triangle. Run the whole episode through your mind and memory. What furniture is around you? How does the floor feel under your feet? Can you usually smell anything as you stand there? What noises do you normally hear?

When you have recreated the red triangle position in your memory, pretend that you are proceeding to the blue circle, and spend a couple of minutes recalling that part of the journey.

Finally, pretend that you have returned to your bed and laid yourself down again.

So ends your first mental cue journey. Establish a regular time each day to carry this out, and astral travel is one step closer.

One exciting day as you carry out the mental cue journey you will experience a peculiar sensation, known as 'bi-location'. You will be aware that you are lying on your couch totally relaxed, yet you will also know that you are standing, looking at a symbol on the wall, in control of another body – your astral body.

Words are blunt tools to try to describe this feeling. You will recognize the sensation with a thrill when it happens. Two separate entities exist, and you are both of them. One lies still on the bed, while the other lives, moves, feels and thinks in another part of your home.

Astral travel is beginning for you.

As you continue to practice, the duality will fade. Your awareness will gradually center on your astral body, and you will no longer be aware of your physical body lying on the bed.

Your full attention, your total sensation of 'being' will be focused in your astral body.

Continue with the mental cue journeys each day until you can confidently lie down, relax, and then find yourself standing in another room, seeing the cue card in front of you.

As I mentioned previously, astral travel depends on your physical and emotional state, and also the phase of the Moon, among other variables. Some days you will lie down and float out of your body in full consciousness in two minutes flat. At other times the whole episode will be less clear, and you may find yourself experiencing bi-location again.

Make a note of your successes, and check on the state of the Moon. You will be able to establish what time of the month is best for you to astral travel.

FUTURE PROGRESS

How you progress from here is entirely up to you. I suggest you proceed slowly and carefully, step-by-step, as you would when learning to master any other art.

If you are learning to play the piano for instance, having mastered a simple scale, you would be unlikely to plunge into an attempt to play a perfect rendition of Rachmaninoff concerto.

Similarly, astral travel is more accurately mastered a step at a time.

VARIATIONS ON CUE TRAVEL

When you are confident of your ability to travel the familiar cue path, add a few variations. Between the red triangle and blue circle positions, stop and look around at the room. Sit down in a chair for a moment. Cross to the window and look out.

If you see anything new outside, make a mental note of it. If anyone is in the room, move your astral body behind him or her – you won't cast a shadow – and see what newspaper is being read, or what page of a book is open.

Then when you return from your astral journey, check those points, as proof to yourself that you have been astrally walking through the other room.

Keep the journeys short at the beginning. Staying out for 10 minutes is long enough for a start.

RETURNING TO YOUR PHYSICAL BODY

Walk, in your astral body, into the room where your physical body is lying. If the door of the room is closed, you should turn the handle – astrally speaking – open the door and close it behind you.

The 'real' or physical door will not open, of course, but its astral equivalent will, and you will enter the room in exactly the same manner as if you were entering in your normal physical state.

Stand inside the room and look across at your body, apparently asleep. This can be a weird sensation, so be prepared for it beforehand.

Your flesh may look greener than you are used to seeing in a mirror, and some people feel a twinge of apprehension as they look at themselves lying there. Cross the room, lie down in your astral body and take up the exact position your physical body is lying in. You will fit into it just like a jelly fitting a mold, or sugar dissolving in coffee.

Once you are back inside, your awareness will merge into your body. Think the words: "That is the end of today's journey," and after a moment of blankness you will find yourself waking up, feeling calm and rested, just as if you have been in a deep sleep.

You will, however, retain a full and clear memory of the journey you have just taken.

EXTENDING YOUR JOURNEYS

Next time you practice, lengthen the journey. When you arrive at your red cue, turn around and walk in your astral body to the front door of your home. Open it in the usual manner and walk outside.[4]

Stroll to the corner of the road, to your mailbox, or to some other familiar point. Check the license plates of cars parked around, look and see who is on the street. See if you can listen to their conversation. Behave, in your astral body, as if you were a tourist in a new town or city. Unlike the regular tourist, you have the advantage that no-one, except strong clairvoyants and psychics, can see you.

---

[4] I mention this opening and closing of doors purposely in your early astral travels. Later, you can drift through doors, walls, people – even mountains.

But at this stage, you have enough new sensations to cope with. Walking through a wall before you are ready for it is often enough to shock you back to your physical body in a hurry, thus aborting the journey.

Extend your walks gradually each day, getting further and further from home.

Next, you will find that walking is a slow way to move around during astral travel. Your mind will take over: decide that you want to visit a friend, and you will be at his/her side like a flash.

Fly, if you wish. Jump your astral body off the ground and soar up, up and away, hovering over buildings and fields, feeling the rush of air in your face, and seeing the ground unreel below you.

Experiment all you please as you gain confidence. If you doubt at any time that it is a 'real' experience, confirm that you have been to some destination by making a note of some specific item or incident, and then later revisit the spot, physically, to check what you saw.

An experienced astral traveler I know in Johannesburg, South Africa goes to the movies in his astral body. He waits until a new movie comes to the city and then takes an astral journey to the movie house. He drifts inside, invisibly, and takes the best seat in the house to watch the movie unreel on the screen.

After which, he pays a visit to the movie in his physical body, paying to go in this time, just to prove to himself that he has seen it before, astrally.

There is literally no limit to where you can fly in your astral body. It matters not how far afield you go: in a single flash of thought, when you are ready to end the journey, you return to your home, and re-enter your physical body as I have described earlier.

WHAT NEXT?

Where can you go and what can you do after you have exhausted the possibilities of astral traveling in this physical world?

There's a whole new world for you to explore – the Astral Planes, or Astral Lights, as some people call it.

No one can tell you, in words, what the Astral Planes are like. The only way to find out is to go there in your astral body. I guarantee that you are in for pleasant surprises which literally have no words to describe them.

Trying to explain the Astral Planes to someone who has yet to go there is like trying to explain the color red to a blind man who has never seen light in color.

Practice, and follow your astral nose. The more you practice, the more fascinating places you will find to explore. Eventually, when the time is right, you will find yourself deeply involved in far more than just traveling the Planes. And what that means, I will leave you the joy of discovering for yourself.

ASTRAL TRAVEL IS SAFE AND ENJOYABLE

Several early books written about astral travel pay a great deal of attention to alleged dangers and fears you can encounter while journeying. One primary question most people ask is: "What happens if I get 'stuck' outside my body, unable to return?"

The simple answer is "You won't!" Initially, your biggest challenge will be to stay 'out'. Frequently, as you discover some new exciting experience, like your first airborne astral journey, the surge of emotion will bring you zipping back to your physical body in a split-second, disappointed that you have returned so soon.

If anything or anyone disturbs your physical body as it lies at home, you will find yourself back inside at once. A ringing telephone, a loud noise, someone calling your name, any emergency, or even a sharp attack of indigestion will bring you back to the reality of the physical plane in short order, none the worse for your infinitely fast trip, except perhaps for a slight headache. Relax for a few minutes and that discomfort will disappear.

I will, however, insert a single caution here. If you choose to astral travel while you are under the influence of any drugs, be it aspirin, tranquilizer, stimulant, marijuana, LSD, cocaine or heroin, you can induce a bad trip. Under drugged conditions, you can open some strange mental doors which can distress you.

Some writers on astral travel refer to meeting dangerous entities in the Planes; others refer to the danger of another soul possessing your body while you are out traveling; some speak of 'breaking the silver cord' and becoming permanently detached from your physical body so that it dies.

Let me take those three points one at a time.

Any 'dangerous entities' you meet can harm you only as much as you allow them to. If you are ever in an astral situation which distresses you, merely think yourself into a brighter, happier situation, and you are there in a flash.

Possession of your body by another soul, under the conditions I have described, is a myth dreamed up by fiction writers and sensationalists who enjoy trying to scare people.

When you astral travel, your awareness is someplace else, but your body is fully occupied and protected by your life force which keeps it breathing and living. As I said before, any interference with your physical body will bring you back home in a flash – and that word 'interference' covers all physical, mental and spiritual influences.

Finally, dying while astral travel is another piece of scary folk-lore.

If your body is in such a weak state that it is on the point of death, or if a physical malfunction such as a heart attack occurs, astral travel is impossible or will be terminated instantly.

At death, the body, soul and mind move into a sequence of events which have nothing to do with conscious astral travel. Astral travel is not a factor in that change of state which we have named 'death'.

You are in no more peril when you astral travel than you are when you enjoy a good night's sleep.

Astral traveling is one of the most fascinating arts of the occult, and leads on to tremendous expansion of awareness. Your first astral journey is but the first step along a road which many others have traveled to their ultimate benefit.

As with several other slightly obscure statements in this book, you will understand exactly what I mean at a later stage of your occult development.

SUMMARY

Astral travel is achieved in several well-defined steps. The method I have offered you is only one of many methods – this one I have found useful and practical for the majority of people who wish to master the art.

Summarized, this method consists of:

1. Preparations. Establish a regular time and a quiet, dim environment for your exercises.

2. Relaxation.

3. Seeing your astral body. Practice this until you can do it with reasonable facility before you proceed to Step 4. Once Step 3 is mastered,

you need to only do it occasionally as you feel inclined.

4. Physical cue travel. Practice this for at least a week, or longer if you wish, before you proceed to Step 5. Once you begin Step 5 you can abandon Step 4, unless at any time you wish to take a 'refresher' course.

5. Mental cue travel. This leads inevitably to full, controlled, conscious astral travel.

There you have the complete method. Proceed slowly and methodically and you will experience one of the greatest occult sensations known to man.

I wish you good fortune in your seeking. We shall meet at the top of the mountain. So mote it be.

Geof Gray-Cobb

Geof Gray-Cobb
Montreal, Canada, 1973

Cue 1

Cue 2

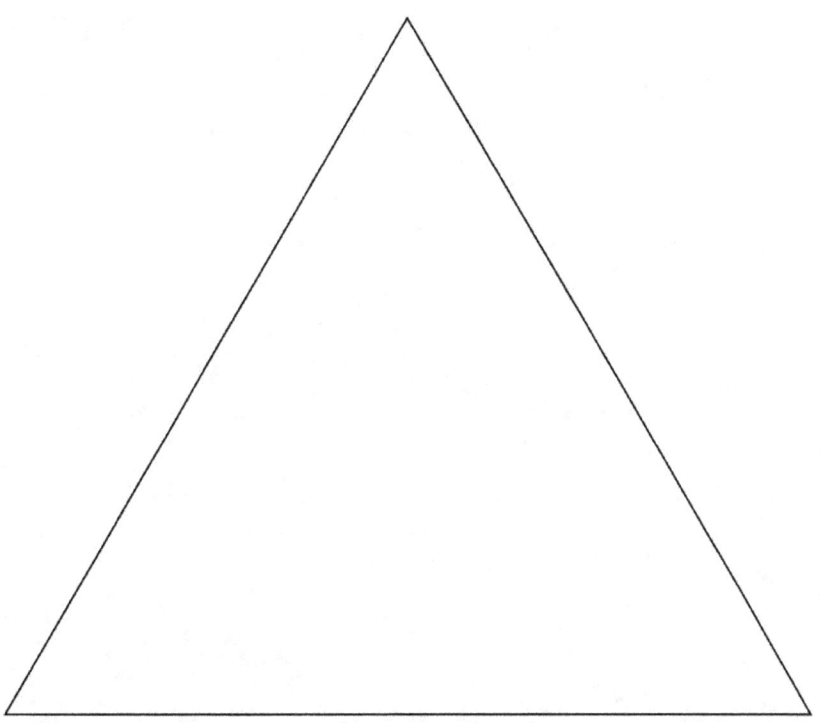

Cue 3

CHAPTER 16

LOVE, LOVE, LOVE

Sun Sign: Libra, Pisces, Taurus

Moon Sign: Using any of the Sun signs under Libra, Pisces, Taurus and Sagittarius are the strongest to attract love.

If we have followed some of this book already, we have learnt that to attract the energy that we wish to feel, we must put some effort towards that. We must be that magnet of cause. To do this we must love ourselves and decide what would suit our own 'peace of mind'. Some will want an independent partner. Some will want a person to spend all their time with. Some will want 50-50. You choose, but before you do, remember that to attract this you must 'want' NOT 'need'. To be needy is to be lonely. This is where the next chapter helps if you still feel that you have not shifted all that needs to be balanced.

THE EAST FACE OF LOVE AND PEACE OF MIND

Taken from *Secrets From Beyond the Pyramids* by Geof Gray-Cobb

Bring out the pyramid and look steadily at the Blue Circle for a couple of minutes, then gently allow your eyes to close. Under some lighting conditions you will see an image of the circle floating against the darkness of your eyelids. Whether or not you see this is not critical: I mention it only as a point of interest and because someone is sure to ask why it happens. It's a purely physical phenomenon and occurs because the retina of the eye gets 'tired' of looking at the color. It's neither dangerous to your sight nor significant to your psychic path.

What we're doing here is simply strengthening your attunement with the *East Face Tide of Harmony and Peace.*

If you should find your mind galloping along a mile a minute as you close your eyes, with worries and troubles tumbling over each other for attention, push them into the background for the moment. Think instead of a calm and happy incident in your life; think about quiet places, peaceful surroundings – the deep woods at dawn, for instance, or the holy quiet of a grand cathedral.

You'll feel some of that peace begin to spread through your being at once. Naturally, how much immediate effect the *Blue Circle of Vayu* has depends on exactly how uptight and desperate you are at the outset. But a couple of minutes a day (or as often as feasible on a less regular basis) spent contemplating the Blue Circle will assuredly work fabulous changes in your outlook.

Keep your eyes closed for another couple of minutes then open them. Move onwards with any of the spells in this chapter. We are working towards bringing in 'love' whether that be for yourself, coming from yourself, or coming from another.

DISPEL LONELINESS WITH THE MAGNETIC PICTORIAL TECHNIQUE

Now we move a step closer to specifics. The Blue Circle technique previously described was designed to bring peace and harmony with no special aim in view. This extension of the method is designed to cure the conditions of those who feel lonely and unwanted.

My advice here is to find a picture of a Buddhist monk. One who clearly is showing that he sits in a meditative state of bliss. If you prefer another picture of anything else that shows 'pure peaceful bliss' by all means use that. Let your intuition decide. Your energy will feel drawn towards the perfect picture.

Carry out the steady viewing of the *Blue Circle of Vayu* as I previously described for you, but before you close your eyes, turn your gaze on the picture you've selected.

After a minute or so of this examination, allow your own eyes to close as before.

Again push away worries or troubles, this time by pretending you're walking along a path in warm sunshine, heading toward a city on a hill. Beside you is a companion, radiating warmth, friendliness and happiness.

Practice that for a full minute (or longer if you wish), open your eyes, and end the exercise just as you did with the previous viewing of the Blue Circle.

Another link is firmly forged in your chain connecting you to ultimate peace of mind. The *Magnetic Pictorial Technique* you've now entertained is duly registered in the book of destiny and will assuredly come true for you as you keep practicing this every day, or whenever it is convenient for you to do so.

As you continue to do this it will change your own energy and attract who is supposed to arrive to spend time with you in this physical plane.

If you can have the pyramid on your desk at work, or in your office at home, all the better. Keep the side that you are working on facing you at all times. I keep mine on my work desk plus one in my window. This method works well for all types of power moves.

CHAPTER 17

ENERGY ENHANCING

Sun Sign: Aries, Leo, Aquarius, Virgo,

Moon Sign: Using this energy under the Sun signs will be the strongest. Leo, Aries, Capricorn, Sagittarius.

> Taken from *Helping Yourself with Acupineology*
> by Geof Gray-Cobb

I highly recommend that if you do not have this book to obtain it. I could have copied all of the helpful tips here in regards to stimulation that the physical body can attract, repel and change through movement. This book is probably the most in-depth and has a completely different content matter for activation of change done with the physical movements.
    I chose only to add the gestures of psinic, pectoral and umbilical fields.
    Using this will be, daily or weekly if you lack time, of great benefit. Keep in mind that we will be creating a yearly program here.
    Broadly speaking, you have three energy fields flowing through your body, each connected with various areas of your life. Each field is made up of currents or *lines of force*; just as a piece of cloth is woven from separate strands of cotton. The lines of force we shall be using flow from and to important, easily located points on your hands and fingers.

Your psinic field

Your *psinic* (pronounced "sigh-nick") *field* flows back and forth between your hands and your face. Its lines of force are associated with all mental processes and are very powerfully concentrated at a point in the center of your forehead about an inch above your eyebrows. That point is your *psinic focus*.

Your pectoral field

Your *pectoral* (pronounced "peck-troll") *field* forms a web of energy between your chest and your hands and is connected with material things that you can see, touch, smell, taste, or hear. A point midway between your nipples is your *pectoral focus,* where the lines of force converge into a forceful beam of power.

Your umbilical field

Your *umbilical* (pronounced "um-billy-cool") *field* flows from the area around your navel to and from your hands. It is associated with abstract concepts, such as spiritual growth, and all other aspects of life which are not the province of the other two fields. Your navel is your *umbilical focus*, where the lines of force unite into an invisible, potent stream.

GESTURES BRING YOUR ENERGY FIELDS UP TO MAXIMUM STRENGTH

All three of the energy fields described earlier flow through your hands, and some psychics, especially those who are into yoga, say they can clearly see the lines of force radiating from the human hand.

By simple placement of your fingers and palms, you can charge up your energy fields at any time, so that when they are called on, they will be fully charged and raring to go to work on your personal miracles.

Fortunately, all three of these gestures are 'natural' ones. You can perform them at any time, without the rest of the world even noticing anything unusual. At any spare moment of the day or night, when you have nothing else to do for a couple of minutes or so, you can use these energy-building gestures. The results, when you call on your iso-bionic energy, will be that much more effective.

Your umbilical gesture

To charge your umbilical field, clasp your hands together and lay your palms flat across your navel. This gesture is performed in precisely the same way as a person who has had a good meal sits back and puts his hands on his stomach, saying, "That was good!"

Try the gesture once and you'll understand what I'm telling you. Of course, you do not have to say, "That was good." You say nothing at all.

As you put your hands in position, close your eyes, relax your muscles, and breathe deeply five times. Return your breathing to its regular tempo and depth, keeping your eyes closed. Two minutes is long enough to hold the gesture. A longer time will not add much to the total power in your umbilical field, but if you wish to continue to hold the gesture, by all means do so. However, do *not* continue to breathe deeply – you'll hyperventilate, taking on more oxygen than your body can easily handle, and you will make yourself dizzy. As a rule, should you find your head spinning even slightly while you're doing any of these gestures, stop the deep breathing at once and allow everything to swing back to normal.

Your pectoral gesture

The technique for charging your pectoral field is very similar to the foregoing gesture. The clasped fingers are identical, except that they are held higher up on your body, across and in contact with your chest, covering your pectoral focus.

You can move directly from the umbilical gesture to the pectoral gesture merely by sliding your clasped hands about eight inches up your chest until they come to rest with the heels of your palms covering your nipples.

Hold this position and take five deep breaths, with your eyes closed and your muscles as relaxed as possible. Hold the gesture for two minutes.

Your psinic gesture

Your psinic field is charged with your hands held in a different position. Bring your open hands up on either side of your head and gently place your thumbs against your cheeks, just in front of your ear. Your fingers should be pointing up and forward. Fold your hands around until your little fingers touch each other and also touch your forehead about an inch above your eyebrows.

Spread the rest of your fingers comfortably and allow them to touch your head. Rest your elbows on a table or the arms of your chair if that can be arranged without difficulty.

Take five deep breaths after closing your eyes and allowing your body to relax. Hold the gesture for about two minutes.

Performing more than one gesture

If you so desire, you can charge up more than one field at a time as you perform these gestures. In such a case, you are required to take five deep breaths *once only*, whether you're charging up two of your fields or all three of them.

CHAPTER 18

CHANNELING

Sun Sign: Pisces, Scorpio, Cancer.

Moon Sign: Under the Sun signs the best energy to combine with is Pisces.

Do not attempt to try to channel until you have done some of this energy work. Then you will hear the correct answers.

Believe me channeling is easy if you do not doubt what you say. The problem is, with many folks, they think about what it is they were about to say and doubt it. Therefore they are never correct. When in doubt that will be what you achieve. Never think the impossible.

Again relaxation is in order. However, for the aspect of channeling, a daily practice of meditation rules here. At the end of your meditation just say in your mind "can you hear me"? You will hear back, "Yes we can hear you". It will be almost like an echo. Some will be distant and some louder. Try to focus in on a frequency so that you can hear in your mind. Make your questions short, as it appears that the energy needed to connect with you is short in power.

Under a hypnosis type of energy you will easily connect. Here are a couple of poems channeled to my folks during their time when the Sunday group gatherings for the evening was channeling. This was the theme of the evening as the group started. I explained to you that my Mother has a twin flame named Louis that she spoke with all of her life. This is from himself.

"For although no incident which is in the past can affect our future, our thoughts impressed on the cells of our body can indeed affect us. We are as we think, and this is the only time a past action can have an effect on a future path – for the reaction of the whole 'I' is built on what has been impressed before."

To All Those Who Seek The Divine Union

Search for the light of reason
Seek in the light of spirit
Dig in the turmoiled stirrings
Of those teachings far beyond
Sleep for the sound of trumpets
Hark to be heav'nly throng
Hold to the evening glory
Feel for the angel's song
Hold to the touch of knowledge
Fly to the clouds above
Float in the arms of spirit
Bask in the warmth of love
Then when the trumpets clamour
Loud in the end of time
Brave are the divine soldiers
As the last long clarions chime.

By LT. Louis F. Hellerman – WWI Fighter Pilot
Born December 24, 1898. Shot down in flames August 15, 1917.
Given to us by automatic writing May, 1970.

The Tide of Divine Union

Thou seekest in the timorous mind – a touch, no more – yet
Less and more than words do pass between thee.
Even as the creaming breakers flood the conscious mind
Then shall ye know in the last reckoning
In the cold clear light of reason swamping all
Logic, ties nor family
Shall stand against this tide.
Deep swells the pending union
And deeper thrusts the knife of a new and stranger pulling
A heart and mind encounter
Crashing like a sunburst
Outwards upwards inwards outwards
Until the carnate beings dwell in splendor on a lonely cloud
Beyond the tiny roils of earth
Tis to be, even as I say
Try as ye may – but with each dawning day
The straining waters lap against the dam
Which, breaking of a sudden,
Sweeps all away
To leave but driftwood jetsam
And the words
I – thou.

By LT. Louis F. Hellerman – WWI Fighter Pilot
Born December 24, 1898. Shot down in flames August 15, 1917.
Given to us by automatic writing August, 1971.

CHAPTER 19

ANIMALS

Time: There is no specific time for this if you have lost a pet. The quicker you use this locater spell the better.

Again as we focus here we will apply the day, month, zodiac sign and time according to the Angel cards.

LOST PET

If you know the birthdate of your pet go through the instructions that show what Angel cards to choose. If not, just choose the day, month, zodiac sign, date and time that you are working this spell.

Take a picture of your lost pet and place him/her in the centre of the altar or space that you have chosen to work with.

Now sit silently focusing upon the picture. As you feel yourself relaxing then close your eyes and call in the Angels that you have put out to help you.

Since this to me is a vital and important area we will call in the most profound God that I have ever brought to help. His name is Doga [Pronounced Doe-Ga]. I only use Doga in dire circumstances. He is not to be bothered for trivial stuff or the material areas.

However once I write that, there will also be someone who will defy this and try it. That is why I wrote the 'reversal' spell so that you could apologise.

Instructions

Once you have called in all your helpers ask out loud for them to locate 'China' as we will call your pet for now. Then bring to your third eye mind area the thought AND sound of your pet. Keep it in your minds eyes for as long as you can. Keep going deeper into relaxation. Stay as long as you feel you need.

One of many things will happen. You will see, in the upper right hand side of your mind, a picture of China and where she/he is located.

You may hear them and in some sort of intuitiveness just KNOW where they are.

More Instructions

If you have another animal in the house make sure that this pet is included in the above calling of the Angels. Then take the animal with you while you search.

Do NOT send the Angels and Doga home until you have finished searching, as they will accompany you. But do not forget. Again the going home words to let the Angels and Doga leave are: ETA MESA EST. Even if you have not found China, under no circumstances curse or deliberately not thank them for their work. Gratitude under all work is heard and appreciated.

If you have not found China with the above instructions then you need to know if the animal has died. For this I would use a pendulum. However, without having used a pendulum before you need to know that it is working correctly.

Here is what happened to me while traveling with a cat that I could not find.

Back in 2001 I was traveling to Vancouver to take my color therapy courses and stopped at my parent's house for the night. At the time they lived in Christina Lake, British Columbia. I had my two cats with me at the time. Lucas who traveled very well and walked as a dog would beside you. Princess who preferred to stay put in the house or room. While traveling there I had stopped at a rest station to eat and let Lucas out for his walk. During his walk, lo and behold, he got stung by a bee. The top of his head swelled beyond belief. I swear he must have been allergic to bee stings. We continued on to my parent's house quite hastily, and once there my dad and I left for the vet. I let Princess out and put her in my parent's house with my Mum staying with her.

Arriving back after having Lucas's massive head drained and a shot given, my Mum asked "did you take Princess with you"? "No, mum I did not" I replied looking worried. I searched the entire house, then the grounds and lastly got in my van and drove around. No Princess materialized. I was devastated, as I knew I would have to leave in the morning as my course started the day after. My mum said "do not worry when we find her we will ship her to you". I had planned to be on the road for six weeks and that did not sit well with me at all.

I had not given up, but I had nowhere else to look. I sat down outside with my dad and both of us were quiet. Suddenly the deeper part of my mind shifted and I turned to my Dad and said "I know where she is" and with almost a hypnotic feeling, that appeared to be dragging me, I was walked to my van. I leaned in, pulled the engine handle release and stepped to the front of the van and pulled up the hood. There was Princess tucked beside the battery looking scared, but not hurt at all. I pulled her into my arms and gleefully called out "I found her". How did I know? To this day all I can tell you is that I had my focus and worry of her so deeply imbedded into my subconscious that I connected with her, and she must have relayed the message either directly to me or through an animal spirit guide that was able to propel me to her. Yes, she stayed in a bedroom with a closed door after that. She also lived to 21 years of age and passed in my arms in 2017.

If you read the last book I re-published I wrote about the experience of my astral traveling. This was the same house. A magic house to be sure. If you can ever sleep in an earth house the experience is well worth it.

SICKNESS IN YOUR PET

Use at any time the pet is ill.

Before you attempt this I trust that you have seen a vet? I trust that you have fed the pet with proper food and not just the cheap stuff that will not keep the animal healthy? If so then forge ahead with this energy working spell.

Keep in mind, just like humans, animals get tired. Sometimes it is their time to leave you. Allow this. Keep the memories of their souls in your heart. Be with them when their time is due. Hold them as they leave the physical plane. You would not wish to be alone, or with strangers when it is your time.

Let us try though to see if the illness will leave. Having said this we set up the place of work. We can use the altar, an open space on the floor or even around the animal if he or she is lying in their bed.

Get the cards ready. We are choosing the day that you are working, the number of the day, the month, the zodiac sign and time, plus if you know the pets birthday their Angel card. Now take your card that has the Leader Group upon it and create the circle. Keep your Leader card standing.

Relax as we have instructed many times, but this time will bit a bit different. Place your hands on your pet. As you relax really feel the energy of the animal. You may feel the heart beat on your hands, maybe a lick from your pet, a stirring of some kind but you will connect as you relax.

Say the Angels names and call them in. As you feel a shift of energy ask "if it is in the best interest for 'name of pet' to heal so be it'. Stay resting with this energy for as long as you like.

As usual we say the words Eta Mesa Est when we no longer need the Angels to be helping.

You can use this daily or even twice a day. This works exceedingly well after surgery or any type of wounds that are healing. In sickness you must allow the animals to choose to accept the healing energy offered.

CHAPTER 20

DREAMS

Sun and Moon signs can be recognized if you journal your dreams and make a note of where the Sun and Moon sit. Then you can decipher what nights will be the strongest for dreaming.

DREAMS AND WHAT THEY CAN TELL YOU

One of the things you may note in dreams is that you cannot lie. The other is you rarely, if ever, can see yourself as in a mirror or reflection. Understanding that dreams are like speaking in a different language. You need to learn this language and most of the time it is shown in pictures and diagrams.

Some people dream strongly every night. This we refer to as astral traveling. Others dream and sometime have recall and sometimes not. Others claim they never dream.

Let's get the 'I never dream' out of the equation here. If you never dream then you are VERY stuck in life. Dreams stop when there is no need to speak to you anymore. When you are simply living a 'ground hog' day as I like to call your days, then you have no growth to them through either fear of change, or whatever you have decided is not worth undertaking.

Those who dream and wake up wondering 'what the heck did that mean' need to write them down. In the future you will be reading them and saying 'wow what strange dreams'. Some of them are clearly related to a TV show that you would have watched, or a game you may have played shortly before turning in for the night. This is often a past life that has been recalled up in your subconscious while watching the movie, show or theme of the game you played. You truly need to write them down in as much detail as you can recall.

Astral traveling in dreams

Now astral traveling in dreaming is a totally different feature. This I have done many times. Sometimes, when I am aware and in my dream I am able to say to myself 'this is a dream' and then take control of it. Then I normally just flap my arms and am able to fly. However, that seems to wake me up after a bit. I also do not seem to have any control as to where I fly.

Next, a dream I took control of was fascinating to me. I still think about it a lot. I am rarely able to see myself in my dreams. I am aware it is me but never see my face. In this dream I am about to tell you about, I looked ahead of myself and saw a body of water. I knew then that if I could get to this body of water I could see myself. In the dream, as I tried to walk, I could not. I then lay down and under me was grass. I dug my fingers into the grass and with extreme pain that was VERY real I pulled myself towards the water. It was long and tedious and very hard to do but I pressed on and tried to ignore the pain in my determination to get to the water. I finally reached the lake and triumphantly pulled myself over to my reflection. Boy was I shocked. I had blue eyes, shorter hair and was absolutely gorgeous. I mean gorgeous. If I look like this in the afterlife man oh man will I be a happy soul. I woke up and have forever recalled this dream. I also am very attracted to blue eyed males. Funnily all of my relationships, except for one, have been with blue-eyed men.

This following dream was on the same trip that I wrote about above when Princess got lost.

My mother gave me her bed in her bedroom. At the time they lived in an earth house. This is a house that is built into the ground.

As I drifted off to sleep I felt my soul moving towards the top of my head. I am assuming it is the soul, the energy that exists after the physical body lets go of us. If I was to explain this correctly I was aware of what was happening, yet asleep. As I got half way out of my crown chakra area I awoke fully. This stopped the action, but then I mumbled to myself "so this is how it's done" and promptly went back to the sleep awareness. The energy swirled and continued out of the top of my head where it flew away. At this point I lost awareness of it. A description of this is about the same as a movement that a worm makes as it goes into the earth. The size is about the width and length of your little finger. It goes upwards to the spot on the top of the head that never hardens. The reason we wear helmets. It picks the exact center of this spot and like I described, twirls its way out and then the energy soars upwards.

I was amazed and knew that this is the way we leave the body upon death. I also know that this is how we go off to our dream state but have the attachment still to the physical energy and that is why we come back. When we are ready to leave we cut that invisible cord and leave the physical body behind.

Where do we go? That I cannot tell you with 100% accuracy. You are free to believe what you like, but I do say to all my clients 'it will all make perfect sense at the end'.

For those who have truly vivid dreams know that if you can come to the understanding in the actual dream that you are dreaming you can take control of the scene. Once you do this, flap your arms and you will fly.

However, some dream powerfully all the time. You will find that many of these people dream about future actions that do take place. Or they dream about an instance that always has a death around them within a month. Either way these types of dreamers are able to be forewarned about things that will take place in the future. If you are these souls do not be afraid of them. Embrace them as life is showing you that the past, present and future has already been set.

One of my vivid dreams was undeniable annoying upon waking. In my dream I won $250,000. Yes, a quarter of a million dollars. I was ecstatically happy and doing a happy dance in my dream when all of a sudden I said "oh no, this is a dream right"? Whoever was there said "no, you are awake, it's real". Then they pinched me and walked me around my home and I was totally convinced I was awake. I mean totally convinced. If you can envision this then you will be able to know how I felt when I woke up and realized that being convinced that I was awake made me the happiest person – having believed that I had won this money. This would be akin to you finding out that you had checked last week's lottery ticket and not realized that you were looking at the wrong date but had all the numbers. Believe me, I recall this dream vividly all the time, but often hope that it was a future prediction. So far it has not been, although I do not lack business and therefore do not lack funds.

Use your dreams to learn a new language. Once you speak that language you can understand the messages you are being sent or observing for your own knowledge. Do not use a book, as that is simply another person's opinion of what their symbols represent. Keep a journal of one word descriptions of the dream and see what the day holds. Add the actions of the day to the opposite side with a few words. Let's say you dream of being stuck in deep water. You write down 'deep water, stuck, me'. That day you get a speeding ticket. Your words opposite are 'ticket, speeding'. You dream it again and sure enough that day you get another ticket. Now you know that on nights you dream the water dream, to either not drive, or slow down and be very careful. You have learnt some words of your new language.

Ending this section off with the opening line you will notice that two things are prominent in dreams. You cannot see yourself, as in a mirror. You cannot lie when asked a question.

PAST LIFE DREAMS

This is exciting when you finally can see the past and how it connects to your life now that will show you where it needs correcting.

Again we will be setting up the intention to allow the subconscious to release the truth of the past. Take your five Personal Angel cards. This time though we are taking them to our sleeping quarters. Along with this I want you to choose three things that you are extremely attracted to. Suggestions would be art work. Do you have a piece of art work that you just had to buy? It does not matter when you bought it, just that you knew you loved it and now it hangs on your wall. Next choose a colored item in your favorite color. It can be a piece of clothing or simply anything that you really adore. Now you need one last thing. A crystal. Choose the crystal that you favor most. Arrange all of this in the center of the cards.

DREAMS

You will now call upon your seven personal Angels that I hope by now you have learnt their names. If not, write them down or just look at the cards. If you know them by heart now is the time to lie back and close your eyes. State their names and ask for them to be present. Use the same wording that you have decided suits the arrival best. If you have not learnt the names by now read them out loud and then lie back and close the eyes. Relax as usual. This time though you are asking the Angels to supply you with visual either 'now' in the mind or as we had intended to, process the dream states in an extremely visual way so that it can be recalled in detail as you awaken.

You will most likely fall asleep doing this. It is the intention and the only time that you will not be able to use Eta Mesa Est to send them home. Do not fret, they will stay the night and help with your request. In the morning, AFTER you have written down your glorious memories, and now know what the program of lessons are here to do upon the physical, you may state the words Eta Mesa Est and do not forget the gratitude. You may wish to write out a little reminder note and put it beside your bed before you activate all of this.

If you do not thank your Angel helpers the purpose is not done with eagerness. Liken it to you being called to help with something all the time, and the same person never ever says thank you. How would you feel when they called? Most likely you would ignore the call display telling you that it is them again. Gratitude is immense.

If by any chance this does not work because you have not relaxed, or you have had a restless night, do not forget to thank them anyway and use the words Eta Mesa Est to release them home. Pick another night and try again.

My past life dream: My oh my!! I was visiting my younger son in a hospital of some kind. We were walking around the grounds and all of a sudden he was shot from behind with a gun and died on the spot. I was devastated. Then the dream moved to the next part.

In this dream my older son was married to the same woman he is married to today in this life. They lived in the southern part of the United States where the big stately homes are built and they had land, servants and obviously power and money. In my dream I kept calling the house and nobody picked up. I then ran into my son's best friend, who in this life is his best friend as well. In the dream I said to the best friend "why is my son not answering" and he replied "because you go on and on about his brother".

The dream was more detailed and in slow motion as I lived through all of this. However!! It matches today and their lives.

My younger son was not the most honest in his youth and stole from me. Without going into all the details, just know that I went on and on about it whenever I spoke to my older son.

Now once my older son got married, his wife wanted a big house and money. She made sure that material was important. She made sure the kids all had the latest IPhones. Whatever she wanted she ran the debt up. You could see the parallel of trying to repeat what she had obtained in the past life. At least I can. However it was not to be. They had to file bankruptcy, not once but twice. Even with a win of $50,000 she simply spent it taking everyone away on a vacation instead of paying off debt.

I did not interfere, but around her you could feel the dislike coming at me. Especially when I had little to offer once moving out here and giving up my past.

My book *Then Now and Forever* by VcToria Gray-Cobb explains my past that I chose to leave.

From this past life dream I knew that I had to shift my way of talking about his brother. I stopped referring to the thefts and stayed away from her.

This dream helped me understand them and made me understand that in that past life I never saw my grandchildren. Today they are back and I spend time with them, but do not make my life all about them as I appeared to do so in the past.

Because of this my life has grown to be not only successful, but super-duper peaceful.

CHAPTER 21

ALIENS AND SPACE SHIPS

Time: This works best if your natal chart has Pluto in the 12th house. You may then do this at any time. If not, then use this when the Moon is in Scorpio. If your natal chart has Pluto in the 12th then double up the energy under the Scorpio Moon.

Sun Sign: Scorpio

If you do not believe in them please feel free to skip this chapter. First I am going to activate one chant in a spell that will allow you to see a space ship.

Remember when I said do not call on Doga to waste his time? This is why. We are now going to use him again. Of all the Gods, Angels and Lords that we call upon to help, he, in my opinion, is the most powerful and will do the bidding, but he is not to be messed with.

Only your Group Leader Angel card is needed here and the name to be called upon is Doga. You must be prepared to really relax here. I need you to be sitting very comfortable in a chair with the Angel card resting upon your lap.

I have not created a card for Doga. When working with him you need to know that he is an almighty powerful energy. Many people pray. I am using that as an example of pulling in energy. When eyes are closed and the hands are in prayer position one is connecting with their God. The same is for Doga. Do not google his name as you will not find him as a

God. He was channeled to me as a powerful energy only to work with outer space and emergencies.

I then need you to utter the name Doga and with an impression of what you feel he would look like. Keep that image in your mind no matter what comes to the visual cortex. Now place your left hand over the Angel card and then chant Doga eleven times. Now ask that in the next 'time frame of choice' [e.g., 2 weeks, 2 months, etc.] you are privy to seeing an alien ship passing overhead. Keep in mind that this would be easier to ask for if you are able to sit outside and view the stars or have some sort of window that allows this. Trust me this works.

I saw my first alien ship passing over at the age of fourteen. I was lying on the grass outside Expo 67 in Montreal, Quebec, Canada. I was staring up at the night sky, and lo and behold this round, disc type, spinning contraption came above me. It moved quickly in circles and then with a rush of speed left the sky. I was not afraid at all. I actually marveled at the sight and wished it had been longer.

Next, in the year 1999 again lying in grass, except this time I was in my back yard. It was not an alien ship but a fighter plane from world war one that came out of the clouds and hovered for awhile. Although this is not what I considered alien, I added it here to show that time has no space. I believe that all time can be seen if you apply the desire.

Lastly, and this happened a few weeks ago. The year is 2020. Do not ask what happened to me as I cannot tell you.

As I was coming to from my sleep, a very loud noise was being emitted from myself. I thought that perhaps I had been snoring loudly and had wakened myself this way. I felt sick to my stomach and had a searing pain in the left side of my forehead. I then thought to myself is it possible I had a heart attack?

Based upon the way I felt I called my doctor just to set up an appointment to see if anything was wrong. I had to wait a month and did not push the issue as I felt fine with waiting. They did say to call back if anything else happened, and I knew I could get in quicker if that was to be.

Then I went to feed my cat who was waiting in her normal spot on my bed, as she likes to be fed there. Oh my!! My cat, my wonderful seventeen year old cat named China, had been shaved on the side of her body. Placed over this area was fur that was not the color of her undertone at all. She is a rag doll so she has very long fur all over. Now she had this section about 3 inches by 3 inches all short with a dark type of fur that was nowhere else on her body.

I was beginning to think this was not any type of illness. My head still raged and as I looked at myself in the mirror, above my left eyebrow, right where my head was raging, were the tiniest, tiniest sized pin pricks. Three of them, each about 1/8th of an inch apart in a row. I kid you not. The entire day I just relaxed and tried not to move my head. The following day the pain was gone, but if I lowered my head the pain came back. On the third day all was well again. I took pictures of the cat, also my head. It is truly hard to see in the pictures the small pin pricks but on my cat it is very visible. What happened to me? I do not know and I have no memory of the night. Nor why it would have happened.

Yes, I saw the doctor and my blood pressure is 'excellent' and as a precaution she will be sending me for a 'stress' test for my heart. After I told her my story and showed her the pictures she also added "but I cannot tell you what happened to the cat nor help her". ☺

I added this story as I feel we would be very close minded to believe that we are the only race within this large space above us. I will always wonder what happened to me that night. Oh and particularly why my cat was with me as well.

This is about all I am writing about. It is my last book. You need no further assistance than to follow this from birthday to birthday or whatever day of the year you have chosen to start. Your plant that you have seeded will tell you how much growth you have attained.

Update on the 'stress' tests for my heart: All of my tests came back as completely normal. I, therefore, have no other choice than to declare it as an abduction. I base this upon the cat and her side being shaved. If all had been normal with China I would have chalked it up to myself snoring and having a bad headache. I cannot though. I do believe that the cat was meant to be shaven in a way so I would believe.

CHAPTER 22

PENDULUMS, TIPS AND ADVICE

A Quick 'Hey I do not have a lot of time' spell.

Anytime of the day or night.

Running late? Have to get out the door? This will take two minutes. Be warned though that when used in a 'quick' way it should be for simple things like 'please find me a parking spot close to work or wherever you are going' 'make the bus be late as I am running late' 'keep me from slipping on the ice' 'make traffic an easy commute' and so on and so forth. At later dates when you have time to use the NAP Relaxation or your own relaxation techniques you can use this for a bigger general purpose.

GENERAL PURPOSE INVOCATION

In the powers vested in Thee, Iaoth, Petahyah and Opiel* I command Thine aid. Bring Thy influences to bear on my affairs. My desire is. . . . . .**

Thou hast heard, and in the Name of VEE-NOKE-OH-TEE-SEE-AWN, Thou shalt fulfil my will in all things which seem good unto me. So mote it be.

* Pronounced EE-AH-OAT, PATE-AH-YAH and OH-PEA-ELL.

** Here, state what you wish to happen. Ask for one thing at a time with this Invocation for best results. If you include a whole string of requests, the Power is spread thinly over all of them, and takes longer. Better to achieve one at a time in order of importance.

THE DIFFERENCE BETWEEN RITUALS AND SPELLS

Rituals

Rituals consist of Magic working in a particular place, using gestures and words in specific patterns, at a certain time. The vibrations produced work with the energies of the Universe, and those energies shape your future into what you want it to be. Rituals work most efficiently when you choose the time and conditions carefully, prepare yourself beforehand and go through the techniques step by step.

Spells

Spells use the same Forces of the Universe, but they rely more on thought patterns then Rituals do. Most Spells can be worked at anytime, anywhere, with little preparation. Their advantage is that they are unobtrusive.

Pendulum Work

If in doubt use the pendulum. However again, just like the Angel cards you must use the same one and enhance it with your own energy. Do not lend it out under any circumstances.

Choose carefully. You may either make your own by purchasing a crystal at a metaphysical store or on line, and fishing line at any craft store.

Buying a pendulum: Pick it up, and in your mind ask for the word 'no' to be shown. If this pendulum wants to work with you it will quickly respond. Moving back and forth, or up and down or in a circle. Now ask again for 'yes'. If it responds in another movement very quickly it wants to be yours. Buy it.

If it takes a long time to move either in a circle or otherwise put it back and choose again. If both motions are the same, for the 'no' and 'yes' query, put it back and choose another.

If you are making your own pendulum, thread the line through the crystal and set it up in the center of your five Personal Angel cards. If you bought it do the same. Introduce the pendulum to the cards by name. Yes, I would name your pendulum. Do you need masculine, feminine or neutral energy added to your life? Choose a name that suits the description of your need.

After the introduction, if you still have to take the Angel cards and sleep with them, add the pendulum to them as well. If you have already done the energy shift for your Angel cards repeat this action with your pendulum. I allow seven sleeps with anything that I am allowing to create magic, miracles and beauty into my life. Seven as I have said repeatedly, is the spiritual number.

WRAP UP

I have left this till last so that you can set up a theme. If you prefer me to set this up for you please go to my website www.alternativeuniverse.ca under the web store and order the *Complete Set Up For The*

Yearly Transition. This will set up all the times for you based on your personal information and when the Sun and Moon is ready to activate. Of course you then do the work that is set up in the book.

As the book has given you all of the instructions and you have chosen to set this up yourself here are the suggestions.

Read the entire book from cover to cover. What attracts you as you read make a note of the page in your journal. The one I have suggested to keep with your magic working room.

Set up an altar if you have room. This is the best way to work. Otherwise use a vision board. Having the two journals is important. I am presuming you have set up an altar and will set the following with that in mind.

Place the journals in your surroundings as you will have epiphanies and wish to write them down.

If you can work at the same hour daily that will enhance the subconscious to program the actions. If not, do not fret.

Make sure you have a comfortable chair facing your altar. Keep the Completed Pyramid on the altar. If you are lucky enough to be starting this on your birthday then wish yourself a Happy Birthday and as you set up the Angels for the **Bifurcated Soul** action [Chapter 3, page 17] make sure you share that information.

Once you have completed that section, as it is useless to continue if you have not, then take the cards and sleep with them. You are now allowing all the Angels to get to know your true energy and what you really want. As I explained, you will be using all of the cards from time to time.

The list of what has to be removed from your life should be done and aptly named 'Now'.

The list of what you will be focusing on to attract should be done. Named 'Destination'

How you place those on your altar is your choice. How you decorate it is also up to you but having a white cloth as a covering is best. Using different color candles that correspond to the Angel card colors is ideal. Using essential oil or incense is an added pleasantry.

Go back to the 'Destination' and take the book and look at the planetary suggestions for the power of activation.

I have suggested Sun signs and Moon signs for the best times. Once you have your list of shifts now you can set the dates to accomplish these. Keep in mind this is a yearly shift and what you are about to change is planted under the correct energies so it grows.

Find all of these times within the ephemeris. That is a book that gives all of the planets locations. Or wait for my monthly posts that give the location of the planets.

I will assume you have done the homework for the time frames and have marked all of the opportune times next to each of the desires in 'Destination'.

I have posted the meanings of Moon phases below. You need to look at your intentions for the 'Destination' and use the Moon phase if it is sitting in the sign that I have suggested.

Meditation daily is a must. Sitting in your chair with your five Personal Angel cards either on the floor in front of you, or on your lap or where ever you feel they wish to sit. Before you go into a meditative reflecting time, call upon the seven Angels, calling the Group Leader first. Do not forget that once you are done meditating to say the words ETA MESA EST. Do NOT forget.

For meditation you only need to use your five Personal Angel cards. If you wish to bring in the day, date, zodiac, month and time of day you may. See which is more powerful but know that sometimes just your helpers would like to be present by themselves.

Now you have your time frames for work. Your time of daily meditation set. Either set your phone to remind you, or mark it openly on a calendar. If you are the type of person who looks at schedules the day prior then so be it. However, you do not want to miss any of the workings. You have programmed the appointments with your Personal Angels, and they have set this time frame in their schedules. Do not waste theirs or your time.

Now get to work.

PHASES OF THE MOON

The symbolism of Moon Phases

New Moon – The Moon is positioned between the Earth and Sun so it cannot be seen from Earth. This moon phase signifies new beginnings.

Waxing Crescent Moon – 'Waxing' means the Moon's illumination is growing, and 'Crescent' means less than half of the Moon is illuminated. This moon phase signifies intention.

First Quarter Moon – Exactly half of the Moon is illuminated and the other half is shadowed. This particular moon cycle signifies decision making.

Waxing Gibbous Moon – 'Waxing' means the Moon's illumination is growing and 'Gibbous' means more than half of the Moon is illuminated. This moon phase signifies refinement.

Full Moon – The Sun illuminates the entire moon. This particular moon cycle signifies release and sealing of intention.

Waning Gibbous – 'Waning' refers to the decreasing of the Moon's illumination, and 'Gibbous' means more than half of Moon illuminated. This moon phase signifies gratitude.

Third Quarter – Exactly half of the Moon is illuminated and the other half is shadowed. We will see the opposite side of the First Quarter Moon. This moon phase signifies forgiveness.

Waning Crescent – 'Waning' refers to the shrinking of the Moon's illumination and 'Crescent' means less than half of the Moon is illuminated. This particular moon cycle signifies surrender.

Some of these visuals are different in certain areas of the world. Do look at the Moon phase for your location and time.

TESTIMONIALS

I have been a practicing sorcerer for 42 years now. I have found that our journeys are deeply influenced by our first readings, inspirations and guidance. No matter where our path leads us, it is our first steps that dictate our direction, focus and empowerment. The works of Geof Gray-Cobb..... Frater Malak was one my first occult "primers". Well written, clearly understandable and most importantly <u>effective</u>. I would encourage practitioners of all levels and paths to acquire this metaphysical treasure. I think everyone will benefit by this tome of practical knowledge. (James Hunter-Ralston)

Good evening,

I'm in your Facebook group, but wanted to email you here. I've struggled for the last year and a half with dating and finding someone compatible who shared my values. I truly felt like there was no light at the end of the tunnel. It all was a huge struggle. I petitioned Elubatel for success in dating and meeting people. After around two weeks, I got the message that I could stop. A couple of days later, a woman I met online pushed to meet. Tonight she came over and my frustration ended. Elubatel answered my request exactly as I petitioned him.

 I'm so blessed by your work and the work of your father. You may share this in your book if it's not too late, but please just use my initials.

J.

It's 1978 and the Mystic Grimoire had just arrived! I was 18. I loved every page of clear patient guidance to a calmer in control human being, I am thrilled that now a new generation has the opportunity to go on the same magical journey that has helped shape my life and still does! (Julia Laverne)